ROANOKE COUNTY PUBLIC LIBRARY
HEADQUARTERS / 419 LIBRARY
3131 ELECTRIC ROAD
ROANOKE, VA 24018

W9-BBP-432

0 1197 0300843 1

NO LONGER PROPERTY OF ROANOKE COUNTY PUBLIC LIBRARY

Earning Your Own Respect

A Handbook of Personal Responsibility

Thom Rutledge

NEW HARBINGER PUBLICATIONS

Publisher's Note

This publication is designed to provide accurate and authoritative information in regard to the subject matter covered. It is sold with the understanding that the publisher is not engaged in rendering psychological, financial, legal, or other professional services. If expert assistance or counseling is needed, the services of a competent professional should be sought.

Distributed in the U.S.A. by Publishers Group West; in Canada by Raincoast Books; in Great Britain by Airlift Book Company, Ltd.; in South Africa by Real Books, Ltd.; in Australia by Boobook; and in New Zealand by Tandem Press.

Copyright © 1998 by Thom Rutledge
New Harbinger Publications, Inc.
5674 Shattuck Avenue
Oakland, CA 94609

Cover design by Poulson/Gluck Design.
Author's photograph by Peter Nash.
Edited by Catharine Sutker.

Also by Thom Rutledge: *Simple Truth, If I Were They,* and *Practice Makes Practice* (audio tape). For a brochure, call (615) 327-3423.

Library of Congress Catalog Card Number: 98-66706
ISBN 1-57224-151-9 Paperback

All Rights Reserved.

Printed in the United States of America on recycled paper

New Harbinger Publications' Website address: www.newharbinger.com

First Printing

This one is for Dede,
my lab partner and my teacher
when it comes to the lessons
of personal responsibility.

Ultimately, man should not ask what the meaning of his life is, but rather he must recognize that it is he who is asked.

—Viktor E. Frankl
Man's Search for Meaning

Nothing can bring you peace but yourself.
Nothing can bring you peace but the triumph of principles.

—Ralph Waldo Emerson
Self-Reliance

Contents

PART II   Getting Practice

Preface

Sometimes after a therapy client has been at the whole self-exploration and personal healing thing for a while, she will begin to show up for sessions without any specific agenda. When she began therapy there was always more to cover than could ever fit inside the hour. Now she is feeling better, generally has no burning issues, and sometimes hasn't the slightest idea what she could possibly have to talk about for an entire hour.

I have been at this place with more clients than I can count. And as a voracious consumer of psychotherapy myself (some by choice and some by necessity), I have personally experienced this interesting lull. Of course, it is at this point the insurance companies and HMOs and PPOs tell the clinician to stop seeing the client—she is all better now. But I don't think so. Experience has taught me to regard these lulls as a sign that things are just about to get interesting. When the therapy client no longer knows what she will say as she begins each session, she no longer exercises control over the goings-on in the therapy room.

The unconscious mind has been waiting patiently for this lull, listening for this particular brand of silence. The unconscious mind slips off its jacket, rolls up its sleeves, pulls up a chair . . . and begins to participate in the therapy. What a troublemaker. What an interesting, turbulent gift.

That's what it has been like writing this book.

My previous books have been collections of ideas, concepts, and practices that were already well rehearsed in my clinical practice, in my workshops, or in the articles that I wrote for my syndicated column. *Earning Your Own Respect* has emerged from the lull. At times, it has felt more like I am reading the book than writing it.

For the past few months, I have once again been that therapy client who has no idea how she can possibly think of enough to say, certainly not enough to fill the whole hour. And once again, a truckload of life's lessons have been waiting for me—even after the insurance companies and the HMOs and the PPOs would have pronounced me "all better."

I want to thank the people at New Harbinger Publications for believing in me enough to back a second book. Especially thank you to Kristin Beck, my guardian angel in the publishing world, and Catharine Sutker, a talented editor with the requisite patience and sense of humor to put up with me. Thank you also to Amy Shoup, Kirk Johnson, Gary Faith, Lynn Woodmansee, Trish Sanders, and as always, Dede Beasley.

My clients and workshop participants are my collaborators in this work, and I can never thank them enough for the opportunity to learn life's valuable lessons along with them—and get paid for it!

If I were to list all of the people who have played a part in my own lessons in personal responsibility (so far), there would not be enough space left for the book. But I do want to thank Janet Samples and Professor Peter Lucchesi for being two people who got the ball rolling.

Introduction

Once upon a time, somewhere near Rapid City, South Dakota, in a place called the Gold Nugget Motel, in a meeting room full of self-help explorers, I heard the author Sharon Wegsheider-Cruse say, "We go to therapy to live. We don't live to go to therapy." I like that idea, and to a large extent, that is what this book is about.

I have been a psychotherapist for more than fifteen years, and I am extremely grateful for having landed in such an interesting, challenging, and rewarding career. I owe much of the quality of my life now to therapists who have helped me along the way, both professionally and personally. One of the most important lessons we can offer the next generation is that knowing how, when, and to whom to reach for help is *strength*, not weakness, and that being aware and respectful of the many aspects of our personality within our "one personality" is wisdom, not an indictment of insanity.

But when we forget that therapy, personal growth seminars, and self-help books are means to an end, we're in trouble. All good things have a downside; psychotherapy and self-help exploration are no exception. I have come to think of therapy, for instance, as having potential side effects just like medication. We want to benefit from the good that can be done but need to be aware of the possibility of counterproductive, even dangerous, side effects. Here is a list of potential side effects of therapy that I give to my clients:

- **Excessive Analysis:** Increasingly needing to understand—and explaining—the meaning of everything.

- **Pathological Fairness:** Being so invested in "owning your own stuff," that you can no longer reasonably hold others accountable for their choices.

- **Process Dependency:** Believing in the adage, "Life is a journey, not a destination," to the point of dropping all expectations to arrive anywhere. Consequently, you don't expect or strive for results; you just focus on one long journey.

- **Therapist Dependency:** Consulting your therapist on all matters of importance; or asking yourself in these situations, *What would my therapist think is best?*

- **The 50/50 Delusion:** Believing that relationship problems have a 50/50 responsibility split always. Never taking full responsibility for a situation.

- **The New-Improved Blame:** Avoiding other people's confrontations of you by saying (or at least thinking), *That's your issue.*

- **Hyper-Jargon:** Speaking in psychological terms (psychobabble) to the point where other people don't want to talk to you.

- **The All-Purpose Excuse:** Using what you have learned about yourself in therapy to justify your less-than-responsible actions, such as *That's just the way I am; I can't help it.*

This book is about avoiding these side effects. It is about not getting caught up in *getting ready to live* that we forget to live. Imagine a football team that becomes so involved in planning their strategy for the big game that they forget to leave the locker room to go on the playing field, or the student who never applies the knowledge acquired from years of study. Psychotherapy, personal growth seminars, and reading books like this one are classroom time, locker-room preparation. The real deal is out there—in our day-to-day, unpredictable lives. The challenge is to live a life that you feel good about, to be the person you choose to be. On your deathbed, when you're 112 or so, and someone asks, "How do you think you did?" Most likely, you'll want to be able to say, "Pretty good I think."

Accomplishing this goal is very much like saving money: You cannot wait until the last minute, or even tomorrow—since tomorrow may *be* the last minute. You have to start now. You've probably heard countless times that if you want to save money, you have to "take it off the top." If you wait for the "extra money" to save, there will be no savings. A *life* that you feel good about will be built out of *days* that you feel good about. You cannot afford to wait for spare time to feel good about yourself, any more than you can wait for the extra money to save. Each day ask yourself, *How do I think I did?* and listen carefully to the answer.

The books I have written have been about what happens—or what I believe needs to happen—*inside* the locker room. This one is about what I believe needs to be happening *outside* the therapy room, *outside* the personal growth seminars, and *outside* the covers of the self-help books. For as much as I believe in what I do for a living, I also believe that we must balance *study* with *application*, and *preparation* with *action*. As important as it is to break through the resistance to reaching out for help when we need it, it is equally important to learn how and when to rely on ourselves. The goal of any good therapy or strategy for personal growth should be to help set us back on our own two feet, to connect us with our own good judgment, to reintroduce us to the one person on this earth who we need to be able to trust above all others. Guess who?

Aligning Your Life with Your Personal Value System

In its simplest form, here is my thinking for this book: To earn your own respect you must live responsibly. To live responsibly you must identify and clarify your *personal value system* and act on a daily basis in accordance with that value system. In other words, you will respect yourself to the degree that you do not violate your own value system. This is one of life's offensively simple truths, something Alcoholics Anonymous refers to as *simple, but not easy.*

I worked as a magician off and on for much of my young life and still throw in a trick or two at my seminars and speaking engagements. When demonstrating sleight of hand with playing cards, I will sometimes show an interested spectator how I accomplish a particular effect. His response is often something like, "Oh I get it. That's simple." And then he attempts to duplicate the moves I have shown him, only to be frustrated again and again with each repeated attempt to follow my "simple" instructions. What he has not taken into consideration is that simple does not mean easy, and that by rehearsing my sleight of hand moves for years, I have created a secondary illusion: that the card trick is both simple and easy.

Taking Responsiblity and Earning Your Own Respect

The same principles hold for the simple instructions for self-respect. Identify your personal value system, then act according to that value system. Presto, there you have it: self-respect. *Oh I get it. That's simple.* Yet, you hold in your hands an entire book exploring the meaning and practice of personal responsibility and self-respect, and the thoughts and ideas herein can barely scratch the surface of all that can be said about such an important subject. The subject of this book in its broadest sense is an exploration of our human condition. More specifically, there are two questions I want this book to introduce or reinforce in your mind; ask yourself: *What do I really want to do with my one human life? Am I doing it?*

Aspiring to Selfishness

Living responsibly requires a lifetime of rehearsal, and a dedicated, even selfish focus on the goal. Ironically, it is our acts of thorough selfishness that will often lead us to responsible lives and self-respect. Certain behaviors we think of traditionally as "selfish" are not, in the bigger picture, very self-serving. For example, the young man who has a gun in the face of the clerk at some corner market right now may seem to be acting selfishly, but his choices will not serve him well. The woman who rushes into a burning house to save children she has never even met will appear to us to be acting "selflessly," when in fact, it is a reflex of selfishness that drives her to the courageous act. Her value system is developed to the point where she knows instinctively that in order to remain congruent with that value system she must attempt the rescue. She is acting to avoid pain—the pain of violating her own value system.

Most of us will not often, if at all, face such dire circumstances in which our values are tested. But in more subtle packages, we are all presented with "values clarification" tests every day of our lives. *To act in congruence with our value systems is to act responsibly, and this will serve us well.* This is the selfishness to which we must aspire; this is the selfishness with which we will earn our own respect.

How to Get the Most from This Book

It has been a long time since I read a nonfiction book from cover to cover, front to back. I like to skip around. I have done my best to write *Earning Your Own Respect* so that you can skip around too if you want. But for those of you who still insist on reading a book from front to back, and for my publisher, who tends to value some sense of order, I wrote it from beginning to end, and it should read well that way.

Earning Your Own Respect is a follow-up to my first New Harbinger book, *The Self-Forgiveness Handbook,* but it is not a sequel. Reading *The Self-Forgiveness Handbook* is not at all a prerequisite for reading and benefiting from this book. I will suggest, however, that if you discover that you're having difficulty separating from your self-critical messages, or if you are not able to recognize and reinforce your successes, you may want to read *The Self-Forgiveness Handbook.* A synopsis of the seven components of self-forgiveness is included in chapter 3 that may help you to decide.

Earning Your Own Respect is presented in two parts. Part I sets the stage with what I consider the essential *foundation* for the fully responsible life; specifically, *open-mindedness* and *self-compassion.* Part II introduces the seven components of personal responsibility. I have identified these components by interviewing clients, colleagues, and friends about what they consider to be the most important elements of personal responsibility. With these notes in hand—along with my own professional and personal biases—I sat down with some colleagues, and we determined what seemed to be the most commonly mentioned characteristics of the fully-responsible person. Here is what we came up with: *self-esteem, congruence, motivation, power, purpose, courage* and *humility.* And so go the names of the themes in part II of this book.

Responding

Writing in a journal as you read *Earning Your Own Respect* can be extremely enlightening. I believe that what I have to say is important—if I didn't I wouldn't write these books—but what you have to say or how you *respond* to what you are reading is infinitely more important than anything I can say when it comes to your life. This book is a resource, not an authority.

Even if you are reluctant to do so, I suggest that you try keeping a journal as you read. There is something about putting thoughts into words and words onto paper that will help you to tangibly discover the challenges that you need to face in earning your own respect. I have discovered that not only is writing a powerful tool to help internalize the material you are reading, but also that having the journal to look back on years later is better than an old photo album. The journal will be filled with snapshots of your consciousness at work.

If you are willing to give journal writing a try, I recommend that you find a notebook of some kind—one that you like the look, size, weight, and feel of. Don't treat it too gently; it is your *workbook*. Write in the margins. Doodle.

I have included sections called *Responding* throughout the book. These brief sections will offer something for you to consider, or ask questions in regard to what you're reading. I hope you will find my suggestions and questions helpful, but don't stop there. Let your journal also be *your* responses to *your* questions. After all, this is a book about *your* ability to respond.

PART I

Building a Foundation

*There's a higher road and a lower road
to any place we want to go.*

—Melody Beattie
Stop Being Mean to Yourself

1

Responsibility 101

Defining Personal Responsibility

Maybe you are curious, as I have been over the past years, about responsibility. Maybe you need some clarification, but your questions are not well formed yet. Maybe your reading this book will turn out to be an act of personal responsibility.

How is one of the primary terms for this book defined? What is responsibility? Who is responsible, and how do we know? Are there objective back-of-the-book answers to these questions, or is our exploration to be entirely subjective? Did you pick up this book because you think of yourself as an irresponsible person seeking to become responsible? Or are you a responsible person seeking an increased—or improved—sense of personal responsibility?

Who are the most responsible people you know? What is it about them that you perceive as so responsible? Do they hold down high-pressure jobs? Do they juggle a career outside the home with being a good parent? Are they reliable? Consistent? Are they responsible because they pay their bills on time? Do they make it a point to always vote when elections roll around?

And what, do you suppose, made these people so responsible? Did they learn it from a parent, or teacher, or maybe a grandparent?

Did they become responsible out of necessity because no one else around them would pick up the ball? Have they always been so responsible? Do they think of themselves as highly responsible people? Do you think of yourself as a responsible person?

Defining Your Responsibilities

To find **the** answers to the questions "What is personal responsibility?" and "How do we become responsible?" is a tall order, beyond the scope of this one chapter. In fact, we will be collecting and piecing together answers to these questions throughout the book—not to mention the rest of our lives. It is important that we not settle for any one or two short or oversimplified answers to questions that can make such a significant difference in our lives. Of course, we will also need to be careful not to make complex what is, in fact, simple.

To begin, in order to establish a foundation for our exploration, let's take a look at personal responsibility from two equally important perspectives: (1) responsibility as it pertains to the many roles that we play in relationship with others, and (2) the meaning of *Self-responsibility*.

Responsibility and Others

Traditionally we think of responsibility in the context of relationship. As I write this very sentence, I am making my best effort to be responsible to my publisher's deadline for this manuscript. I have just taken a break to feed the dog breakfast and then let her outside so that she won't act irresponsibly on the carpet. In doing so, I am being responsible *to* the dog, and *to* my wife since we share the duties of taking care of our pets. As a psychotherapist, I am being responsible to my clients by showing up on time for appointments and by being a good listener and co-problem solver. I am sometimes unreliable about things, like calling my mother on a regular basis when I say that I will at the end of every conversation we have, and remembering my friends' birthdays on time. In this way, I am *not* acting responsibly.

We're all very experienced in thinking of responsibility in this way, so this is the easy part. In one of my seminars, I ask participants to take a few minutes to consider themselves solely within the context of being people who are responsible to other people. The next instruction is quite simple: Make a list of the people *to* whom you are responsible. The following lists are examples from participants in a recent seminar. This first list from Seth, a man in his early twenties, shows who he feels most responsible *to*.

- Parents
- Grandparents
- Girlfriend
- Little brother
- Boss
- Co-workers
- Friends

Next is Leah's list, a forty-five-year-old woman from the same seminar.

- Husband
- Two daughters
- Granddaughter (two months from now)
- Employer (ad agency)
- Colleagues (work team)
- Assistant/secretary
- Parents
- Husband's parents
- Nonprofit agency board of directors (member, officer)
- Students (creative writing class)

A New Perspective

Take at least ten minutes to look at the list you've made. This may be a list of people you were already aware of, with no surprises. But you may see something there that you hadn't thought about before. For instance, Seth, the man in his early twenties who made the first list, said that he had never before thought about how many different people he was responsible to. He described himself as feeling overwhelmed after spending only a couple of minutes reviewing his list.

Leah, the forty-five-year-old woman who made the second list, had a different response. After taking the suggested ten minutes to sit with the list and experience her feelings and thoughts, she returned to the seminar group with a broad smile, jokingly throwing her shoulders back in an exaggerated position of pride and self-assurance. Everyone in the group was most curious about her, so she reported her response first:

Before tonight I have never thought of myself as "responsible." I haven't thought that I was irresponsible either; I just have never stepped back to see what I see when I look at the list I just made.

I can feel the negative messages pushing in right now as I am speaking. They want to minimize what I am saying, but it's not working—at least it's not working right now. As I look at this list and think about the many responsibilities that I have to everyone on my list, I would have to be blind not to see that I am, after all, a responsible person. I do a lot of things for a lot of people. I don't think I have ever given myself even a small pat on the back for that.

The people on my list can count on me. And they do.

Spontaneous applause, cheers, and a couple of shrill whistles followed. It was clear to the others in the seminar that this woman had just taken a giant step forward. And the best part is that she took that big step simply by slowing down and taking a look at herself from an angle she had not previously considered.

Responding

Take a few minutes and make your own list.

Spend a few more minutes thinking—or making a few more notes—about the responsibilities you have to each of the people, or groups of people, on your list. For the time being, don't worry about whether or not you're doing a good job with your responsibilities.

Keep in mind that this is an entirely subjective exercise; there are no right or wrong responses. Read over the list a couple of times. Try reading it aloud. I have heard several people say that reading their lists aloud made them seem more real, or more legitimate. Then, just allow yourself to consider what you've written, listening inward to your responding thoughts and feelings. Do your best to remain an observer of your responses, allowing each thought and each feeling to have its say and then allowing it to move on. I use the image of a receiving line, with me standing in a doorway shaking hands with each feeling and thought that comes through. My job is to acknowledge each one and to keep the line moving.

You may discover that you have more to add to your list. Feel free to do that, but I caution you to not avoid the "quiet time" with your list by continued writing. Your list doesn't have to be "complete"; you can always add to it later.

After your five- or ten-minute contemplation, write a paragraph or two about your responses. If you're working in a group, you may or may not choose to write first and then share with the group or to share spontaneously about the experience.

Responsibility "for" Others or "to" Others?

There is a small matter of prepositions that we need to discuss here. The prepositions in question are "to" and "for," such brief little words, but oh what an impact they can have on our lives. There is a significant difference between being responsible *to* someone and being responsible *for* someone. Think about this in terms of your list. Read through your list, interchanging the two prepositions. Read, listen, and feel the following examples:

I am responsible **to** my wife.	I am responsible **for** my wife.
He is responsible **to** his infant son.	He is responsible **for** his infant son.
We are responsible **to** the ficas tree.	We are responsible **for** the ficas tree.
Dan is responsible **to** his seventeen-year-old daughter.	Dan is responsible **for** his seventeen-year-old daughter.

Can you see the difference? More important, can you feel the difference? The point here is not to get lost in semantics, but to clarify the two different *natures* of responsibility that are expressed with the simple change of a preposition. To be responsible *for* someone or something is to be responsible for its well-being, and possibly its very existence. It is the most direct of relationships and is best exemplified by the relationship between a parent and an infant. Infancy is a condition of total dependence, and the mother, father, and other adult caregivers are correspondingly in a position of total responsibility. The infant's well-being, and his or her very life, is appropriately the responsibility of the adults.

Responsibility "for" Others

But how often have you felt responsible *for* another adult in a relationship—believing, or at least acting as if, you were responsible for that person's (remember, a full-grown adult) feelings, thoughts, choices, and actions? Many people grew up in families in which the unwritten and unspoken law was that the children are responsible for the adults. For example, some children may feel responsible for the following scenarios: *Mom's depressed again because we are such difficult children to raise. I should have been able to do something to stop Dad from getting drunk again. If I don't get into that college, I'm not sure my parents can handle it.* These same children, made to feel and act as little adults, eventually grow into adults who will very likely feel responsible *for* the other significant adults in their lives. After all, that's just the way it has always been; it's what they know.

Take another look at your list. Circle the name(s) of anyone on your list that you have felt—or feel—responsible for inappropriately.

Before we move on to *to,* let's take a look at the example of Dan and his seventeen-year-old daughter. This is an interesting example because it confronts us with lots of gray area regarding his responsibilities. Is Dan responsible *for* his daughter? Since she is not yet eighteen, the law would say that in many ways he is technically responsible for her. She is likely still living at home with her parents, and so we could say that even though Dan is a long way from being responsible for her every meal being a nutritious one, as he was when she was an infant, he continues to be responsible for providing food for her to eat and, of course, shelter under which she can sleep. (Anyone who has ever been a parent of a teenager knows that they are only at home to eat and sleep anyway.)

But even those responsibilities are not clear-cut. What a parent is and is not responsible *for* when it comes to older adolescents (in a variety of circumstances) could no doubt fuel many hours of heated discussion. I have witnessed some of those discussions in my office.

For our purposes, however, let's take a look at what happens to the "responsible for" as the infant becomes the toddler becomes the child becomes the prepubescent bundle of confusion becomes the adolescent becomes the young adult. Quite simply, this is what happens to it: In a relatively healthy family, the "responsible for" moves from *total* to *nonexistent* over the time it takes for the infant to become an adult. This doesn't mean that parents' responsibilities with their children diminish, then disappear, but instead that "responsible for" makes its transformation into "responsible to" over the course of the child's development into adulthood.

At this point, I feel responsible *to* you, the reader, to tell you more about what it means to be responsible to someone or something.

Responsibility "to" Others

Responsibility *to* someone or something is significantly different. Here, we are looking at a relationship that is more contractual and limited in nature than the all-encompassing responsibility *for*. That is not to minimize the magnitude and importance of such relationships; often these are some of the most important relationships in our lives. The most important distinction to be made is that responsibility *to* implies a contract between equals or, in transactional analysis terms, an adult-to-adult transaction.

I am not responsible *for* my wife, but my responsibility *to* her is a governing force in my life. Although this does tend to dilute the romance in the telling, consider it this way: Dede and I have a contractual agreement that isn't particularly complex, but it makes up a significant portion of the foundation of each of our lives. In brief, we count on it. We trust it. And we expect that the contract will be honored. This is an essential point: *We expect the contract to be honored.* That is, we expect each other and ourselves to behave in accordance with our marital contract. This is an adult-to-adult agreement, in which neither of us accepts responsibility *for* the other, but in which we both commit to being responsible *to* the other, in the form of behaviorally respecting the contract.

In fact, this description suggests a particular way to define adult-to-adult responsibility agreements. In these agreements, each person commits to act in accordance with a contract—explicit or implicit—that exists separately from either person's essential well-being.

On the Job

Your relationship with your boss or work is in danger of operating according to the same dynamic just described. Jim, a thirty-six-year-old client of mine had been coming to weekly therapy sessions for six or seven months when he began describing his feelings about his job. Jim loved his work, it was his passion, but he hated his job, and as he continued to describe the relationship dynamics in his work environment, it was easy to see why. I told him, "In light of what you're describing—the game playing, manipulation, and back-stabbing—I would say that hating your job is a completely sane response. If you weren't frustrated and dissatisfied in those circumstances, you'd be crazy."

In another session, when Jim said that he wasn't feeling very "sane," he reminded me of what I had said and asked me to explain. This is what I told him:

> *When people decide to explore what makes them tick, and in that process decide to make some changes, to drive up the entrance ramp to the freeway of conscious growth (I am nothing if not corny), many of them are surprised (some more, some less) to see how different the once automatically accepted world around them looks—and feels. And when your point of view changes, so will your responses.*
>
> *Basically, you are* going sane. *You're waking up to a new way of perceiving not only yourself, but your environment as well. And you often don't like what you see from your new perspective. You don't like it because it is not very likable. You may see all the game playing at the office, and even if you were previously aware of it, your tolerance has decreased. And you see some things in a significantly different way. Specifically, what you once accepted as the b.s. that "went with the job" now appears to you more clearly for what it is: inappropriate and abusive relationships. You are awake. You have a new perspective, from which you can see better. You hate what you see. A totally sane response. You are going sane. Congratulations. Feels crappy, doesn't it?*

Jim rolled up his sleeves and dug into the work his new awareness presented to him. (At one point, as he was getting up to leave a session, Jim said, "No wonder this is the road less traveled." I'm still laughing at that one.) Jim discovered that he felt almost totally dependent on his job. He was telling himself that he had to have *that* job, that if he lost that job, no one else would recognize his talents and hire him. And he was absolutely sure that he couldn't succeed financially if he worked independently—even though working for himself was his dream.

Remember, Jim *loved* his work and *hated* his job. Because of his personal value system, Jim felt it was right to follow through with his commitments, even if he wasn't happy. However, he also valued quality of life and desired a life that felt meaningful and fulfilling. This only increased his dilemma with his job. He didn't perceive himself as being capable to accept full responsibility *for* himself and change his circumstance. Whether or not Jim used these words—and he didn't—he was acting as if "the job" was responsible *for* him, that he would not be okay without it.

Simultaneously, Jim was feeling responsible for his boss, the man who had hired him. I pointed out to Jim that in our sessions, he was talking as if his boss could not survive his departure. This is an all too common and strange phenomenon that I call *codependent arrogance*. It's not the kind of arrogance where you get to think how lucky the world is to have you, but instead this kind of arrogance only points to your ability (a highly exaggerated, if not fictional, ability) to create damage, leaving only destruction in your wake.

What Jim needed to learn—and did in relatively short order—was that both his relationship with his job and his relationship with his boss were adult-to-adult relationships and as such involved responsibilities *to* the person and *to* the contract, but that his well-being did not depend on this particular job and that he wasn't responsible *for* his boss's well-being. Jim did have contractual responsibilities in these relationships (professional and personal), and he needed to honor those responsibilities.

Eventually, he did this by having a long, honest talk with his boss and by giving his employer a month's notice when he decided it was time to strike out on his own. In honoring his responsibilities to his job and his boss, Jim was also doing some long neglected, much needed healing: He was honoring his responsibility *to* himself by recognizing *his* role in his unhappiness and then taking the actions to change his situation. Jim took on the responsibility of *acting* on upholding his personal value system.

Caution for Potential Side Effects: If you understand the distinction between "responsibility for" and "responsibility to," I wish you great success as you apply this concept to your personal growth and healing. But please remember that the purpose here is to convey an idea that will be useful to you, and that is the only purpose. You will discover, as I have, that if you get lost in the semantics of the various applications of these prepositions, there will be many exceptions to what I have said, and plenty of plain old confusion. My advice is to *let it go;* use what is helpful here, leave what is not.

Approaching Self-Responsibility

One of the benefits of being a writer is that I can buy all kinds of interesting books and call them business expenses. One of those books is the *Dictionary of Word Origins*, and in it is the etymology of the word "respond," which comes from the Latin "respondere," meaning "promise in return." (Ayto 1990) I like that.

I like the idea of thinking of responsibility as a contract, an exchange in which I am both giving and receiving. In this way, responsibility isn't about some burden that has been placed on me. Instead, it is about keeping the balance, fulfilling a promise. How many times have we tried to explain responsibility to children in this way—you know, the old "privilege comes with responsibility" lecture. But just because we are teaching it that way doesn't mean that we get it. As Richard Bach points out in his wonderful book, *Illusions,* "We teach best what we most need to learn" (Bach 1977). There is one particular aspect of personal responsibility to which this nugget of wisdom applies for almost all of us: self-responsibility.

Double Standard

In order to approach self-responsibility, you need to learn to recognize and respond to your own needs; this is why it's important to examine the double standards operating in your life.

Megan was a pastoral counselor who came to me for therapy. When she sat down to begin her second therapy session, there was something intangible about her, maybe a subtle facial expression, maybe that ever elusive "vibe," that told me she was feeling very discouraged. I was barely settled in my chair when she began:

> *I felt great after our session last week. Well, I felt great for a little while anyway, probably about four or five hours to be more exact. That night I sat down with my journal to write, as you had suggested. [Megan had told me in the first session that she had at one time enjoyed keeping a journal and that she believed it was beneficial.] I did what you said: I made a list of people in my life for whom I had accepted responsibility. I felt guilty writing the list, like I was being egotistical for saying that I had taken responsibility for them. But I stuck with it, I made the list . . . and what a list! By the time I was finished writing, I thought I would have a severe case of writer's cramp, and I was feeling so completely overwhelmed. I felt buried so deep that I thought "I'll never dig myself out of this one." It was actually difficult for me to breath. And even though those feelings have lifted a little, that's pretty much the way I am still feeling.*

Megan's second therapy session was extremely productive. What I had asked her to consider at the end of our first session was how completely, and effectively, she had accepted responsibility for others in her life, while almost as completely and effectively ignoring her own needs. Most of us who struggle with excessive self-criticism will adopt a *double standard,* through which we can see the greater potential of others, but not our own greater potential. In this way, we become extremely close minded—often in the name of what we think is humility. Megan told me that she had read several books about codependency and showed no surprise at my observation, but as we began the second session, something had sunk in that hadn't previously. For whatever reasons (who knows what really determines when we are ready to absorb something new), Megan was no longer just "reading about codependency" or superficially agreeing that she did much more for others than she did for herself. "Something had clicked," she said. That something had clicked while she was making the list in her journal. She had, at least for the moment, lost a significant amount of her tolerance for self-sacrifice, and consequently, she was in real pain.

Not enjoying it anymore

Her predominant experience of feeling "overwhelmed" was not Megan's underlying emotion; it seldom is, for any of us. When we feel overwhelmed, we are experiencing our consciousness' effort to *block* the pain, to shut us down so we don't have to feel anything. The other thing that being overwhelmed can do is keep us distracted and confused enough that we are not able to hold our focus on anything for long. Our consciousness often reacts this way to protect us; if we don't challenge these reactions, they form patterns, sometimes called *defense mechanisms*. We are surrounded. Megan felt surrounded.

Megan's real pain was a seemingly (to her) bottomless pit of despair, involving intense feelings of sadness and loss. Among other things, she was feeling the loss of what had never been, for the life she did not get to live, for the childhood she had to set aside before it even had a chance to exist.

In subsequent sessions, Megan and I worked toward specifying what overwhelmed her. I knew from previous experience (professional and personal) that "overwhelm" never wanted us to look too closely at it; it takes its strength from the ability to appear enormous and remain vague and ill-defined. Once you do look closely, *The Great and Powerful* (and intimidating) *Wizard of Overwhelm* becomes the tangible, and not-so-frightening, *Man Behind the Curtain*.

In a way, Megan's feeling of being overwhelmed made sense. There was much to be avoided. She discovered that when it came to learning how to identify and respond to her own needs, she was starting at square one. She could fairly easily accept, in theory, the need to confront her life-long double standard and the need to "take lessons" in how to take care of herself (learning to balance responding to her needs with those of others). In practice, however, Megan continued to spend plenty of time feeling overwhelmed and, at times, discouraged to the point of wanting to give up.

What she didn't know, until much later, was that by that time, she had worked her way well past what I think of as "the point of no return"—that invisible line we cross when we have become too aware to turn back and succumb to the denial, or at least to turn back with any degree of comfort.

↗ Here, just past the point of no return, Megan—and you and I—are challenged to explore the idea and practice of self-responsibility in ways we have previously been able to sidestep. With heightened awareness, self-neglect and self-denial become increasingly uncomfortable, as they should, in order to nudge (and sometimes push) us toward change.

No wonder this is the road less traveled.

A Scandalous Top Priority

Are you responsible *to*, or responsible *for*, yourself? The answer, as is so often the case with "either/or" questions, is *yes*. No matter how long your list of responsibilities to and for others may be, your greatest responsibility remains the same: *the one and only you*. If you are at all like many of the workshop and lecture audiences I have spoken with, various objections to this thinking will be springing to mind just about now.

How can you say that a parent's greatest responsibility is to herself? What about doctors and nurses? What about the mechanic who works on the 747 on which I will be hitching a ride home tomorrow?

Take a few minutes and write down some reactions (objections or otherwise) of your own. Don't just read; talk back. Argue. But try not to dismiss what I am saying just yet. Stick with me.

I realize that the concept of *putting yourself first* in this way can be difficult to see as having anything to do with being a responsible person. Difficult, that is, as long as we are looking through the lenses of our cultural upbringing. At first, saying that you are your own top priority can sound like the realization of everything you have ever been taught about what is bad and what is wrong with our world. I want to suggest the opposite: that by *not* making ourselves top priority we are participants in a much bigger problem, and that as we learn to turn this big problem around, we will see ripple effects in all sizes—small, medium, and large—depending on the size of our willingness to risk change.

Exploring the Middle Ground

For many years, I was a practicing alcoholic who specialized in the treatment of alcoholism. I loved my work and took it very seriously. And I was good at what I did. However, while I was able to help many people into recovery for *their* alcoholism and other drug dependencies, I continued to practice *mine*. Of course, the characteristic denial associated with all addictions was hard at work, keeping me convinced that I wasn't an alcoholic, that I was different from those I treated. But I was no different.

What's wrong with that picture? I can't say that my drinking never affected my job performance (in the form of hangovers or lost productivity), but I can say that I was, for the most part, a responsible, creative, and energetic employee. Was I being unfair to the clients I treated? The answer, again, is *yes.* I have learned in the dozen years since my most recent drink that by being honest with myself about my own problems and by doing what it takes to face and deal with those problems, I am a much more effective clinician. But that doesn't negate the fact that I was a good therapist before my recovery began. To characterize me, before I acknowledged my problem with alcohol, as *an irresponsible person* or *an irresponsible therapist,* would not be accurate. The characterization of me as *responsible person and therapist* would not fit well either.

The truth is neither black nor white. In those years in which (as my favorite description goes) *I treated by day and drank by night,* I was both responsible and irresponsible. Looking back on that period in my life nearly fifteen years later, with that amazingly clear 20/20 hindsight, what seems most important to recognize is that I was nowhere near acting as responsibly as I could. Let's just say that when it came to personal responsibility, I was working way below my potential.

Therein lies the problem: *working below potential.* And within the description of any problem are the makings of a solution.

I could always find Band-Aid fixes whenever my employers might have reason to "wonder about me." You never saw such fancy footwork (or have you?). I would focus my energy on taking care of somebody else's agenda; I would do something to make the boss happy, and temporarily the problem would go away. You see, I would respond to threats that the truth might be discovered by increasing my active *responsibility to someone else,* while effectively side-stepping any introspection that might lead to my accepting more responsibility for myself—other than doing what I could to insure the safety of my job (in the bigger picture, another Band-Aid).

The central principle running throughout my work—and this book—is this: *As I face the problems that need solving in my life, I will do well to translate each of those problems into a challenge to improve my willingness, capability, and even my potential, to actively accept full responsibility for myself.* A secondary, but essential, principle is that *My concept of personal responsibility must remain open to constant growth and change.*

If this chapter has done its job (notice how I lay the responsibility off on "the chapter"), you will be left with more questions than answers. Gathering good questions is often more productive work than trying to answer them. But we'll find plenty of answers too.

Responding

Read back over chapter 1, and make a list of unanswered questions that seem important to you. Leave space in your journal below each question so that you can make notes later.

Periodically, as you continue to read, return to your unanswered questions to make notes, revise, or add to the questions, or to list various responses.

2

The Open Mind

Learning to Respect
What You Don't Know

I never much cared for Sigmund Freud—until recently, that is. Educated and trained to be a psychotherapist, I based my anti-Freud sentiments on what most of us base our prejudices: *ignorance.* Not just any ignorance, but a particularly powerful (and potentially very dangerous) ignorance characterized by two key elements: *laziness* and *generalization.* Rather than seeking any credible information about Dr. Freud, I opted for the much easier approach of accepting hearsay (the opinions of authors and speakers I have been exposed to through the years) as fact and then assuming that the information I possessed was an accurate representation of the whole man and the entirety of his work. In this highly effective way, I was able to reduce the man and his work into a simple, easy to understand, two-dimensional—never mind, completely erroneous—caricature.

As preparation for writing an article about the client-therapist relationship, I decided to offer myself a sort of "refresher course" in the history of modern psychotherapy. When I began reading about the life of Sigmund Freud, I was surprised to discover a man, and a professional, who refused to fit into the nice, neat, negative package I had so carelessly constructed for him. Where I had anticipated finding an example of egotism and irresponsibility, I found someone who acted quite responsibly, even when others around him did not. Where I had expected to find a target for my outrage at irresponsibility, I found a role model for diligence and integrity. And perhaps most important, I once again found myself in a position in which confronting my own lack of responsibility was the prescribed course of action. *No wonder this is the road less traveled.*

When It's Right to Be Wrong

Here is something I have heard my wife, Dede, say to her therapy clients, to friends, to me, and to herself: *We must be willing to be wrong so that we will eventually be right.* I think this is a wonderful way to remind ourselves of how important it is to remain open-minded as we bob and weave our way through life. Once we dig our heels in and become invested in "being right," reality takes a backseat to our need to defend a position. We all know people who, above all else, have to be right. We all know people who, even with the best of intentions, jump to conclusions and put roots down. Some of us *are* those people; and we have all been those people at least some of the time. I certainly have been—my apologies to Dr. Freud.

Overcoming Your "Knowns"

The basic philosophy of one who is open-minded is this: *I know what I know, I don't know what I don't know, and both of these conditions are constantly subject to change.*

One problem that we face as we work to open our minds is that most of us have been taught to equate "being right" with "being good," and "being strong," and "being smart," when at least as often as not, the opposite is true. The smart man is more likely to be the one who acknowledges what he does not know. The strong woman is the one whose self-esteem does not hinge on "being right," especially in contrast with someone else's "being wrong." And as near as I can tell, simultaneously "being right" and "being good" is a completely arbitrary matter. To become the open-minded people we want to be, it's essential that we bring to the surface, and identify, these old beliefs. Then we must challenge those beliefs, find the loopholes in them, creating the opportunities that we need to broaden our view of the possibilities.

All of this begins when we discover *how we are wrong* and learn to respect the tremendous potential of *not knowing.* As long as we insist on holding tight to the "knowns" in our lives, we remain in a contracted state, generally characterized by a generous layer of rigidity, covering an even greater depth of fear. From this contracted state, we defend our so-called "knowns" because we mistakenly believe them to be necessary for our survival, or at least necessary for our sanity.

Responding

For a day or two, make a special effort to recognize how you respond to not knowing and/or to discovering that you are wrong about something.

Listen for the various opinions from your inner committee, and make some notes.

For now, just let the power of awareness work for you; don't worry about changing anything. There's plenty of change to come.

I suggested this exercise to a man named Brandon with whom I was working on the identified problem of a loss of self-esteem. His responses to the exercise are characteristic of what many of us will find: an airtight closed mind when it comes to negative beliefs about ourselves.

Brandon told me that he didn't need a day or two to know exactly how he responds to not knowing or discovering that he is wrong about something. His response: self-criticism, and plenty of it. "The strange part," he told me, "is that even though the self-criticism is ever present, it really had not bothered me until recently. That's a big part of why I called for help."

I learned that Brandon had always lived with intense self-criticism, but in his own words, he had "learned to ignore" the persistent negative appraisals and predictions that ran constantly, at least during his waking hours. When he showed up in my office, something had changed. He was no longer successfully ignoring the familiar self-criticism. In fact, he was crumbling under the pressure of it. Experiences associated with being wrong or not knowing something were becoming increasingly detrimental to his self-esteem, and he was becoming discouraged and depressed.

The obvious starting point with Brandon was asking the question, "What is different now?" In other words, what has changed between the time when he could ignore self-criticism and when he began to feel haunted and harassed by it? Brandon and I initially came up with several possible contributing factors. He was thirty-eight years old—we wondered if he might simply have become exhausted by the many years of "ignoring." After all, we all have our limits. We also thought that his nearing the treacherous fortieth birthday could have something to do with it. Brandon had recently been considered for, but not offered, a promotion at work. We wondered about that.

Any and all of these circumstances in Brandon's life might have been, and probably were, contributing to his self-esteem backslide. But there was something else, a major change: Approximately six months prior to Brandon's beginning to feel the pressure of his self-criticism, his father had died.

Here is a brief synopsis of what we came up with in our collaborative effort to solve Brandon's problem:

> *Brandon's dad was a "self-made man," and he reminded his son of this often. He was consistently critical of Brandon, but the unspoken agreement between the two of them was that since his dad's intentions were good (to help motivate his son), Brandon would not complain or object. In fact, the more we talked about this in therapy sessions, the clearer it became to both of us that Brandon had learned to accept his father's criticisms as expressions of love and acknowledgment—expressions of love that were silenced when his father died.*
>
> *Brandon missed his father. (Their relationship had consisted of more than just criticism.) And when the possibility arose, in one of our sessions, that Brandon had unconsciously dealt with his loss by no longer ignoring the self-criticisms, his face lit up like the proverbial idea light bulb.*
>
> *Like his father's, Brandon's intentions were also good. He had lowered his guard to self-criticism as a way of trying to comfort himself, a way of filling the void his father had left, a way of keeping a part of his dad with him.*

Brandon's father had not been able to teach his son the value of living in the expanded state of open-mindedness. He could not teach what he did not know. He had responded to the circumstances of his own childhood (one of considerable neglect and deprivation) by "pulling himself up by his own bootstraps," becoming the self-made man Brandon knew as Dad. The mistake this father made is one that many of us make: assuming that since he had succeeded in transforming his circumstances, since his way had worked, then his way was the right way. Brandon, however, was about to learn that there are many ways to define success, and that his father had lived his entire life wearing blinders.

Learning to Listen to Your Inner Voice

Don't confuse *open-mindedness* with *vacant-mindlessness*. I am not advocating that we all become wishy-washy, opinionless airheads, with what a friend of mine calls "The Gilligan Syndrome." My friend is referring to a scene in an episode of the *Gilligan's Island* television series (probably scenes in several episodes) in which each of Gilligan's fellow castaways offers an idea about how to solve a particular problem. As Gilligan listens to the very different, and no doubt outrageous, ideas, he nods his head in vigorous agreement to each and every idea. "Yes, yes, yes, yes, yes," he says.

To be in the expanded state of open-mindedness is to be flexible, not spineless. It is to be enlightened, not blinded by the light. The open-minded person is not a person without independent thoughts and opinions; he is simply remaining aware of the open-minded credo: *I know what I know, I don't know what I don't know, and both of these conditions are always subject to change.* The open-minded person is the person who, no matter how strongly she feels and thinks about something, always does the one thing her close-minded counterpart just as certainly does not do: *She listens.*

Listening is the very essence of open-mindedness. I don't mean "hearing." I mean genuine listening. And the key to genuine listening is curiosity. To listen with curiosity is to listen without preconceived agendas. When we listen with curiosity, we are acknowledging that we don't necessarily know what the other person is going to say to us. And when we listen with curiosity, we remain in a receptive state, rather than retreating to our inner conference room to begin developing a reply.

Brandon's father was not a good listener. He wasn't curious about who Brandon was. Instead, his focus was on "being listened to." In his well-intentioned arrogance, he became what I think of as a *One Way Talking Machine,* a person who is only interested in being heard and not at all interested in listening. A *One Way Talking Machine* will pause now and then in conversation while another person speaks, but when *The Machine* begins to talk again, it is obvious that he was only tolerating the other's voice, not listening to it.

Brandon's father was such a good *One Way Talking Machine* that he was able to create a satellite of himself in Brandon's consciousness, a little part of himself who, masquerading as Brandon's own thoughts, could provide constant critical evaluation and make nega-tive outcome predictions ("You're going to blow it again") any time and any place.

Brandon, on the other hand, had become an expert receiver for the *One Way Talking Machine,* and he continued to act as that excellent receiver even when his dad was not around. And what does an expert receiver do? He listens, he believes what he hears, accepting *The One Way Talking Machine's* messages as gospel truth. In other words, the receiver learns to be closed to possibilities other than what he has been told; the ability to think for himself atrophies. And this is especially true for messages that have to do with self-perception. Brandon could much more easily see someone else's potential beyond any self-limiting beliefs than he could his own. In this way, Brandon was living the old double standard.

The Expert Novice

As Brandon and I explored his self-perception, I noticed that his view of himself was very much aligned with the view that he imag-ined his father had of him. Unfortunately, that was a pretty negative self-image. The father's criticisms were intended to guide (and at times, push) Brandon toward success and away from failure. The unintended result of the constant criticism was Brandon's perception of himself as a failure.

For Brandon's father, *not knowing something* or *getting it wrong* were mortal sins. No matter what success "his way, the right way" brought him, he still missed out on countless opportunities to learn, to grow, to expand—not to mention to get to know his son.

During the course of his therapy, Brandon became able and willing to step outside the bounds of his father's beliefs. Most nota-bly, Brandon learned to perceive great potential in not knowing something, and even in getting it wrong. He practiced what is known in Zen as *beginner's mind,* based on the simple principle of "The expert has nothing to learn, the beginner has everything to learn." When being actively engaged in the process of learning is a part of our definition of success, discovering what we don't know and mak-ing mistakes become essential to our achieving that success.

Brandon began referring to himself as an *expert novice,* taking pride in his new openness to greater possibilities. He even wrote a letter to his dad, telling him what he had learned and how good he was feeling. I had a good laugh when Brandon told me that he had mailed the letter, addressed to "Dad, / c/o The Infinite Universe." Talk about expansive.

Closed and Open Communication

Since *listening with curiosity* is essential to achieving and maintaining our desired state of open mindedness, let's take a closer look at listening in the broader context of communication. Specifically, let's look at how we communicate when we disagree with one another.

Listen to adult human beings in conflict. Listen to their communication. Think about how your parents resolved their differences, about how you communicate in a conflictual situation, about how conflict is handled in your work environment, even about how politicians communicate in an election year debate.

Turn on your television and flip through the channels, keeping one question in mind: *What do I notice about how people who disagree with one another communicate?* Check out a few minutes of *Hard Copy, Sixty Minutes, Geraldo Rivera,* or *Larry King.* What do you notice?

Not long ago I gave this assignment to a therapy group I was working with. I asked the eight members of the group to watch some TV and to write down some of their observations about conflict communication. Television shows like these provide an exaggerated example of communication problems that we've all experienced in different degrees. Here is a sampling of the observations they brought to the next group meeting:

- People talking but not listening

- People talking at the same time, one trying to override the other

- People looking for (and taking advantage of) opportunities to take "pot shots" at one another

- People condescending to other people, by tone of voice, sarcasm, facial expressions, and body language

It was an easy, and very interesting, night of work for me. The group got into a lively discussion not only about what they had observed on television, but also about their own frustrations with conflict communication. They gave me permission to make a few notes as the discussion went on; here is some of what they had to say about themselves:

"It's exhausting to continually attempt honest and respectful communication only to be shut down by someone who is either not capable or not willing to reciprocate."

"It's difficult to avoid digging my heels in, trying to be right, when I feel like everybody is trying to tell me that I'm wrong. It seems only natural that I fight back."

"I hate conflict. I avoid it at all—or almost all—costs."

"My husband and I fight like an episode of a talk show. To listen to us, you would think that we hated each other. And the only thing we accomplish is feeling worse about ourselves and about our marriage. Neither one of us is stupid, but you wouldn't know it to hear us argue."

"I argue a point just like my father did—like a good lawyer devoted to the cause. I'm not proud to admit it, but when I enter a conflict, winning is everything. I guess it's a good thing I'm in therapy, huh?"

I asked the group what they thought underlay their ineffective and/or avoidant styles of conflict communication:

"For me it's a protective instinct, pure and simple. Neither of my parents ever respected what I had to say. I put that armor on early in life, and I still wear it, at the slightest hint of conflict."

"Fear."

"Determination. When I argue, I 'm usually sure that I'm right. And I'm not ineffective. More times than not, I win the argument."

"I don't ever feel like I win. If I have to argue, the feeling underneath is desperation. At times I feel like I'm fighting for my life—or at least my last shred of dignity."

The Most Common Human Error: Sticking to Your Guns

The people you will find in a therapy group like the one described above will tend to be more introspective than the average Joe or Josephine on the street. Because you have chosen to read a book like this, you too are most likely rather introspective. I think we may learn more about how individuals in our society tend to handle differences by watching, listening, and reading the multitude of media sources that surround us these days. Recently, in response to my observations, I wrote a letter to the editor of the local morning newspaper in Nashville.

Dear Editor:
Do we want to solve problems in this country or do we just like to

argue with each other? It certainly keeps the adrenaline flowing. Whether we are watching election year campaign ads or the latest sensational talk show television flap, it seems that we are a population of finger pointers and cry babies desperate to be right. *Right about what? I am beginning to think that "the what" doesn't really matter to us all that much. Just as long as I am right and you are wrong. It's the new-improved American Dream.*

Open debate and conflict for the purpose of creating solutions serves us all. But without a shared dedication to problem solving, we inevitably fall prey to what might be the most common (and deadly) human error: Polarization.

Once the problem is identified, we take a stand (as quickly as possible), we dig in, plug our ears, and open our mouths— endlessly. From my polar extreme I scream at you at your polar extreme. We call each other names, and we hurl broad accusations. But as long as we stand this far apart, we couldn't hear each other accurately even if we were listening.

Exactly what am I talking about? Take your pick: the abortion debate, government spending, the latest Washington scandal, foreign policy, and so on. It's not *what we are talking about that is the problem. It is* how *we are talking. Please think about it.*

Thom Rutledge

More "How" Than "What"

Couples I work with in therapy sometimes become frustrated with me because I don't pay very much attention to the *content* of their problems. It's not unusual for someone to look to me expecting that I might better explain to his wife that *he is right.* (This is not gender specific, by the way. Everybody wants to be right.) But these people don't need a third party listening to their differences in order to tell them who is right and who is wrong. That approach only adds fuel to the fire. Instead, I listen for *how* they communicate, listening from the premise that *effective communication will most always lead to a resolution of the problem.* I suggest that couples come to therapy not for a single fish (one problem solved), but to learn how to fish. I want them to learn to pay a little less attention to the content of their disagreements and a lot more attention to the process—the "how" of their communication.

Communication between human beings, whether it is on a global level or is over the kitchen table, requires the same basic skills and attitudes. When I first found myself in the ominous (and ill-defined) role of "consultant" to managers in business settings, I felt very shaky, fearful that I had stepped outside the arena of my knowledge and my ability to help. My clinical supervisor (with quite a lot of "consulting" experience) assured me that I had not. And to my relief I soon discovered that he was right. Other than the occasional need to disguise myself by wearing a necktie, the work was the same. I listened to *how* people communicated and helped them to increase their interpersonal effectiveness by teaching them the basics. Oh yes, I did discover that business executives often responded better to proposals that said things like "interpersonal effectiveness" rather than "talking to each other better." And that was okay; "interpersonal effectiveness" sounded pretty good when I combined it with wearing a tie.

Teamwork

Thanks to Brandon (my client who was struggling with his self-critical messages), I have found that being the *expert novice* is frequently preferable to being the *expert expert*. Another way I have come to think of this is to imagine my *novice-self* and my *expert-self* working together as a communication team. Although my expert-self (or *knowledgeable-self* may be a more accurate term) may have important contributions to make in the course of a conversation, my novice-self should always remain in charge of listening. As an expert novice I am full of curiosity, and I have plenty of room—and a desire—for new information. As the novice listens, he passes the information received on to my expert- or knowledgeable-self, who will consider the information and formulate a reply. This communication team will be effective as long as each team member respects the other to do his job. Specifically, the expert does not push in to speak while the novice is doing his job. As oversimplified as this may seem, it boils down to learning how to take turns. I guess we didn't learn it all in kindergarten after all.

We must each accept the responsibility to work out our own "inner teamwork," discovering the ways that will work for us, ways that will help to balance our ability and inclination to *impart* information with an ability and inclination to also *gather* information.

Communication 101: Tools for Effective Relationships

In couples therapy there are two phrases that I repeat more than any others. They are: "Slow down" and "Take turns." To be an open and effective communicator, we must master both of these. There are a few more basic principles of effective communication that are just as simple, *and* extremely powerful.

I organized seven of those principles into a concise handout for the couples I work with. I call it *The Communication Starter Kit*, and I will include it here.

Begin with Commitment

Do you remember what it's like to learn to drive a standard shift car? Or to play a musical instrument? Or ride a bicycle? At first the task seems impossible, far too complex to ever be coordinated from your one body and one mind. But with encouragement and lots of commitment and clumsy practice, we do begin to learn.

Even with our 20/20 hindsight we cannot identify exactly when we cross that invisible line from practice into knowing. But we do. We learn. And one day we recognize that what once seemed impossible has become natural, even automatic.

Learning communication skills is no different. Keep in mind that as we learn to act and speak differently, we are also learning to *think* differently. And that is much more difficult than driving a standard shift car.

Mastering new relationship skills is not for the faint of heart. Effective communication—especially in times of conflict—calls for a focused dedication and repetitious practice. It calls for honest self-evaluation, humility, a sense of fair play, and a willingness to change *according to the needs of the relationship.* And it takes (at least) two.

Changing outdated, ineffective communication patterns involves a great deal of *unlearning,* a much greater challenge than simply filling in the blank slate. (Ever try to ditch a bad habit?) In a word, learning effective communication skills calls for *commitment:* commitment to yourself, to your partners in communication, and to the relationship as a whole.

The Starter Kit

What follows are seven important tools to help build effective communication. As with any tools, the first challenge is to learn how and when to use each tool (a hammer is very important, but I don't want to use it to repair my eyeglasses). Keep in mind that this is just a *starter* kit. You will hopefully be adding to this collection of tools for the rest of your life.

The Tools for Communication

1. Take Turns. Two separate agendas can seldom be accomplished at once. Establish some ground rules to insure that you take enough time for each of you to talk while the other is *really* listening.

2. Give Information. State your perceptions and your feelings concisely and respectfully. Avoid *selling* "your side" as the gospel truth, even when it feels that way to you. To resolve any conflict, room must be made for at least two different perspectives. And remember that emotions are *subjective* information, not open for debate (such as, "You shouldn't feel guilty" or "You have no right to be angry").

3. Gather Information. You have a responsibility to do your share of listening, being receptive to what your partner is saying, without immediately judging and categorizing. Ask questions with curiosity, like a good interviewer. And—here comes the radical part—*listen* to the answers. Too often we ask questions not to gather information, but just to make a point.

4. Problem Solve with Benevolence. Be certain to clarify your intention (especially in conflict communication) as seeking a satisfactory outcome for *both* of you. Find common ground on which to base your communication (such as, "We each want to be heard completely and accurately" or "We need to make a decision about . . ."). Avoid seeking agreement about perceptions or feelings as a communication goal. There must be room for both of you to win.

5. Future Orient to Problem Solve. Those who forget the past are, in fact, doomed to repeat it. True. But those who won't let go of the past may also be contributing to its repetition. In conflict communication it is best to state complaints about past behaviors clearly and concisely and then to *future orient.* That is, sink most of your energy into describing or requesting what you want or need from your partner *beginning now.* You must be willing to take the chance that your partner wants to and can change along with

Continued on next page.

you. (If you aren't able to muster any faith that your partner is willing or capable of change, you're probably not working on the most serious problem in your relationship. Get some professional help.)

6. Take Breaks. Each of you must have the authority to call *time out.* And each of you must learn to respect time-outs when they are called. Call time out when you recognize old, dysfunctional patterns of communication taking over (they seem to have a life all their own). When you call time out, it's imperative that you initiate a time to talk again later. Don't just leave it hanging.

7. Backtrack. This is my favorite tool, probably because I use it so often. All progress is not forward. Sometimes the best you can do is stop mid-mistake, apologize, and ask for an opportunity to try again (*do overs,* I believe we used to call them). But be careful to not ask for that chance if you don't think you can follow through with some new and improved communication. If you're not ready yet, try apologizing and backtrack to step 6: Take a break.

Remember: Practice makes . . . practice.

Looking at Your Communication Styles

Whether it's my shortsighted thinking about Sigmund Freud, conflict taking place on television or in our own living rooms, whether we have panned back to take in the global scheme of things or we're focused on our immediate surroundings, whether we are in the therapy room or in a corporate boardroom, we are encountering a universal problem: *ineffective communication.* And ineffective communication is as much—or more—a problem of the contracted mind as it is of a dearth of specific skills.

Think about how the following characteristics affect your ability to communicate:

laziness	gullibility
stubbornness	arrogance
self-righteousness	fear

negativity	ignorance
cynicism	rigidity

Then consider these:

curiosity	fairness
flexibility	discernment
courage	optimism
knowledge	humility
energy	realism

We *all* have *all* of these characteristics, and of course, many more. Depending on an infinite number of variables, we experience every one of them. To maintain an open mind, it's essential to recognize these qualities in yourself. To deny your wide open human potential for all that is good, *and* for all that is bad, is to restrict your capacity for the kind of effective communication that you need in order to bring about real and lasting change—in your personal life, and in your global community.

Responding

Make a short list of some characteristics, some positive and some negative, with which you most identify.

Make some notes about how these characteristics tend to affect your communication skills.

It is important to distinguish between recognizing your *potential* for negative and *acting* in negative ways. If you fool yourself into believing that you act in positive ways because you are only a positive, or good, person, you're—ironically—selling yourself short. That is, you will not be giving yourself due credit for making ethical, constructive choices. Instead, you'll be viewing yourself as a victim (someone who has no choice) to your own goodness. Conversely, you might consider someone who acts unethically or irresponsibly as a bad person who "should be good" instead of seeing that they need to learn to make different choices or take responsibility for acting in positive ways. Sadly, you will then see yourself in that same light when you make ineffective or destructive choices.

Trusting Yourself

Years ago I participated in a professional training program to learn something of the art and the science of *neurolinguistic programming* (NPL), an approach to helping cognitive and behavioral change by directly intervening with how a person's consciousness makes choices about how to interpret himself and the world around him (Bandler 1981). I doubt seriously that the experts in the field of neurolinguistic programming would consider that an adequate definition, but it will do for our purposes. The training I received during that time in my early career has proven extremely valuable for a number of reasons, one of the main benefits being a simple and powerful lesson I learned about choice-making.

The lesson is this:

> *Given the choices available to a person's consciousness at any given time, that person will always make the best choice.*

Sounds strange, doesn't it? Initially it sounds naive and idealistic, not to mention inaccurate. Once it was explained to me, however, it became one of the most positive and hopeful ideas I had ever come across.

Making the best choice, given the choices available, doesn't mean that we will always make good choices—far from it. What it does mean is that our consciousness is always searching for the best option available. Unfortunately any one of our perceptions of what is best is the product of our previous experience and the resulting "programming." This is a highly subjective process. Brandon's dad, for instance, made many of his life-affecting choices based on a belief system that told him that *not knowing* and *being wrong* would place him in an extremely vulnerable state. In order to avoid the danger associated with being so vulnerable, he chose to deny his own fallibility.

Brandon, on the other hand, discovered that he didn't necessarily believe that *not knowing* and *being wrong* were signs of weakness. In our therapy sessions, he was able to reinforce this latent thinking, empowering it to move to front and center of his consciousness. Brandon was able to also replace the fear of vulnerability he had learned from his dad with his own belief that being vulnerable is not necessarily a state of weakness; in fact, in the realm of human relationships, the ability and willingness to be vulnerable is more often than not a strength.

Once Brandon was able to discover within him previously undetected beliefs and construct new beliefs more personally relevant, he began making different choices about how to interpret himself and others. Once he was aware of better options, he took them. Eventually, he learned to trust himself to make good choices, both cognitively and behaviorally, and when he thought he was not making such good choices, he would return to the drawing board with the goal of expanding his options.

Responding

Write about a belief that you have changed in your life and how that change of thinking has affected you.

Write about a belief you currently have that you perceive as restricting you.

Beginner's Mind

No one is totally open-minded. I'm not even sure that would be such a good idea; I think being completely open-minded could make it pretty difficult to function in our day-to-day world. We have to censor and discern the overwhelming amount of information and situations we face constantly. Of course, that might just be a limiting belief of mine. Maybe, if I do my best to remain open, I will change my mind about that before I finish this book. I'll let you know.

For now, remember the simple zen idea of *beginner's mind.* Don't be so unrealistic and close-minded as to expect yourself to be open-minded all of the time. Set your sights on expanding your awareness of all that is around you and within you. Beware of contracting your thinking in response to perceived threats. And be gentle with yourself along the way.

3

Self-Forgiveness

Forgiving Yourself and Moving On

Self-forgiveness is not a snazzy, politically correct, psychobabbling, fashionable way to let ourselves off the sharp hook of accountability. In fact, I think that truth lies in the opposite direction: Self-forgiveness is a crucial step toward becoming a fully responsible adult human being. For many of us, self-forgiveness is the first step, our first responsibility, because without it we are in danger of sinking into the quicksand of our self-absorbing negative thinking. If you doubt this, consider the amount of time and energy that you have spent in your life being self-critical, or even self-condemning, and ask yourself how that time and energy spent has made you a more responsible person. In brief, self-critical thinking is irresponsible.

I am not talking about healthy critical thinking, commonly known as our conscience, that serves to keep us within the bounds of our personal value systems. And I'm not talking about healthy critical thinking that's a part of the feedback system that helps us to learn from experience. The self-criticism I am talking about is that voice inside our heads that consistently tells us we are falling short, that we are never good enough—the voice that even when we succeed at something is quick to remind us that we *should* have succeeded earlier or that we surely won't be able to maintain the success.

The Should Monster

This is the voice that I call *The Should Monster*. Whether the shoulds are explicit or implicit, these are the deeply embedded messages that keep us from taking the next important risk or knock us back down when we dare to get up. These are the negative messages that will interpret even our greatest triumphs as failures, or at least as failures waiting to happen. Here are some examples of The Should Monster at work:

> *You should never had agreed to be the team leader; you can't do it.*
>
> *You should have suggested someone more capable for the job— you're not creative enough.*
>
> *Why didn't you speak up—volunteer to help for a change? You could have been the team leader if you weren't so lazy.*

With The Should Monster, you're a loser no matter which way you go. I have used the metaphor of The Should Monster in therapy and in my workshops for many years, and I know one thing for certain: Neither you nor I will ever do enough or be enough to bring the approval and praise of our Should Monsters.

And yet, like the typical codependent relationship (based on the principle of *whatever you think of me will determine how I feel about myself*), you can become so invested in pleasing the unpleaseable that you become caught in an endless (and useless) struggle to satisfy The Should Monster. Even if you're an outwardly strong, independent person, you can fall into a habitually submissive relationship with The Should Monster.

The time and energy spent in this dysfunctional inner battle is probably time and energy *not* spent in the ways that you choose. I have never known anyone to say, *Oh, good, I have some spare time. I think I will sit down and beat myself up a bit.* Although you do not consciously choose to do so, you may criticize yourself a lot.

Even in the extreme cases, someone who feels compelled toward a self-destructive action hurting her- or himself is not an act of clear *choice.* The conscious desire is to be relieved of pain, and too often this may feel like a choice with only negative options: to endure emotional pain that we are convinced we cannot survive, to continue to experience the shame and guilt associated with our habitual self-criticism, or to cause ourselves physical pain that will distract us from choices one and two. Ask anyone with a history of physical self-abuse (behaviors ranging from exercising when injured to more violent acts such as cutting or hitting oneself). They will tell you that they perceived the physical pain as preferable to the alternatives of overwhelming emotional pain or relentless self-condemnation.

Ultimately, the time and energy expended in self-criticism, self-condemnation, and self-abuse is time spent in self-absorption. Granted, this is self-absorbed pain, but the focus remains constantly on the self. Excessive and relentless self-criticism makes us *less*, not *more* responsive to the world around us. Without self-forgiveness, we remain lost in our own maze, with no way out of this isolated state of existence.

Responding

In what ways have you had a codependent relationship with your Should Monster?

Consider times in your life when you may have opted for one pain to avoid another.

What risks were you ultimately avoiding?

Too Much Humble Pie

Do you know someone who apologizes incessantly, someone who seems to be "sorry" for just about everything? I have known many of these hyper-apologetic individuals over the years, and even while I am feeling compassion for them, they really get on my nerves!

Of course when you confront someone with their constant apologizing, what do they do? Yes. It's a reflex: they apologize.

I think of these as people who have had too much humble pie, and their extreme submissiveness makes an excellent, highly visible example of how excessive self-doubt and constant self-criticism *do not* make for an unselfish life. Once again, the opposite is true: the constant and predictable apology insures that any conversation will quickly become about them. Maybe you are the incessant-apologizer. If so, try not to be too discouraged (there is no need to write me a letter of apology); this behavior is just one more of the multitude of bad communication habits we are all in danger of picking up. The problem is completely resolvable.

Several years ago, I worked with a young man in therapy who had apparently eaten too much humble pie. His name was David, and he apologized for everything. On one occasion I was considerably late for one of our appointments. I apologized for my blunder, but David would have no part of it. After quickly rejecting my apology, he began to apologize to me. His apologies went on for what must have been five minutes, and my pointing out that I was the delinquent one in this case was only fuel to the fire. David's apologies that day were many and varied, but the theme seemed to be that he saw my being late as a predictable indication that I was very busy (and important) and that his being at the office for his scheduled appointment was probably just an inconvenience that I was putting up with, being the magnanimous guy that David saw me as being.

Exhausting. Completely exhausting. And whenever I attempted to explain to David rationally that he had nothing to apologize for, I would become noticeably frustrated, which for him was his cue (as was everything) to apologize.

Now that I think about it, I could have explained to David that I am very important and busy and that it would be very helpful to me if he would continue to send a check for his weekly sessions but stop interfering with my schedule by showing up for the sessions. I wonder how he would have responded?

David and I could talk about many areas of his life during his therapy sessions, but it became clear to me before long that as long as David insisted on apologizing for his very existence, he wouldn't be able to make the slightest change. He was too absorbed in his shame, guilt, and sub-zero self-image to be able to focus on anything else. Oh sure, he would seem to pay attention to other people and situations outside of himself, but inevitably his focus would come rushing back to how inadequate, or stupid, or foolish, or whatever he was. Ironically, for someone who perceived himself as undeserving of attention, he was constantly (indirectly) demanding attention.

Negative Arrogance

David was experiencing what I call *negative arrogance*. It's not the fun kind of arrogance, where you get to go around thinking about how lucky the world is to have you. This is a pain-focused—maybe even punishment-focused—arrogance that says, "I am different from everyone else. I am different in that I am worse than everyone else. Essentially, I am bad news, but in a unique way."

I often ask clients with negative arrogance if there are, in their opinion, other people on the earth who are as useless, or as bad, as they are. Surprisingly, these very intelligent people often tell me the answer is "no." Somehow I have become the lucky therapist who gets to work with the world's most useless, or most stupid, or most inadequate person on the earth. The strange part is that in the course of one day at the office, I might meet with two different individuals who claim to be the most useless person on the earth. Who am I to believe?

A Little Too Much Pie for Us All

You don't have to be the worst person on earth to identify with this problem of negative arrogance. We all get stuck there from time to time, though admittedly, some more than others. The challenge is to not mistake negative arrogance for genuine humility.

When we can recognize negative arrogance for what it is—an obstacle to accepting personal responsibility—then we are ready to learn how to lift ourselves out of the quagmire, back onto the road to personal responsibility.

Responding

How have you been negatively arrogant?

What is the most productive thing you can do when you realize that you are stuck in negative arrogance?

Confronting Your Self-Critical Messages

You must learn to forgive yourself in order to claim full responsibility for yourself. I emphasize this because the vast majority of clients and workshop participants I have worked with have resisted self-forgiveness more than anything else.

Compared to facing the challenge of self-forgiveness, admitting to alcoholism, a failing marriage, problems with the kids, and even excessive self-criticism is simple. I have no idea how many times I have said, in one form or another, to a client, "If you think you can change your life for the better and still hang onto your negative self-perceptions, you're wrong. Eventually, it comes down to a trade: Give up your beliefs that you are bad, less than, undeserving, incompetent, doomed to failure, and you will be given the opportunity for a new and improved life.

You cannot be in that new and improved life as long as you hold onto your negative arrogance—it is no different from any other arrogance. You will have to put it down if you are serious about being happy. Imagine that I am a police hostage negotiator, talking to you through the bullhorn, negotiating the release of yourself.

Disagreeing with Your Should Monster

Letting go of well-rehearsed, long-held, negative beliefs about yourself is not easy. It is very hard work; but just because something is difficult doesn't mean that it can't be done.

It does mean that letting go of your belief in your previous negative self-perceptions will call for a strong, committed effort on your part. Your goal will be to *disagree* with the negative messages, not necessarily to be rid of them. Your Should Monster may always be there with an opinion, but it's possible to take your personal power back from him. Then, when he tells you how you haven't done something well enough, you can glance in his direction—recognize him for The Should Monster he is—and say, "Thank you for sharing. Now sit down."

This is a tall order, so please be patient and supportive of yourself as you move in this direction. In other words, beware of The Should Monster who will criticize you for not doing a "good enough" job of standing up to your Should Monster.

Self-Forgiveness and Personal Responsibility

Forgiveness isn't so much something you do as it is your natural state when you aren't holding onto old resentments, pain, fear, and guilt. When you harbor ill will, resentment, and unexpressed hurt for others, it is your responsibility to find a way to express and release the feelings—not only for the sake of the other person, but for your own physical, mental, and emotional well-being. Whether finding expression for those feelings results in something you call forgiveness is irrelevant. The point is that "constipated emotions" will sooner or later become toxic to you.

The vast majority of stored negative emotions that you have when you begin to take a close, accurate, and honest look inside, are feelings you have about yourself. These are the most toxic emotions of all.

Constipated toxic emotions are like powerful magnets that attract negativity and repel positive charges. Consider David again, who had such a pervasively negative view of himself that he could only perceive himself as constantly at fault. He had a long history of relationships with people who would try to rescue him from himself, but until he became committed to doing the hard work of identifying and letting go of his negative arrogance, nothing was going to change. He experienced the same negative patterns in relationships over and over again. Later, in his therapy, I remember David calling it "God's perpetual re-tests."

And as for David's low self-esteem repelling positive energy, people he met who were at least adequate in taking care of themselves would soon recognize the quicksand surrounding David and choose to step away. Of course, David's Should Monster would make excellent use of such times by telling David that the person going away was just one more piece of evidence that he is worthless and will always be abandoned by others.

Self-Forgiveness As Realism

I have been working with the concept of self-forgiveness long enough that I no longer think of it as the act of forgiving oneself as much as I think of it as an overall attitude, or even a philosophy, toward ourselves. I consider the goal of this self-forgiveness work to be the establishment of a daily practice of self-compassion.

To be self-forgiving, or to practice self-compassion, is never about elevating yourself to some pedestal or declaring yourself "forgiven." I think of it more like washing dishes. I feel great when the dishes are all washed and put away, but I know that in a matter of an hour or so (or maybe minutes) there will be more dishes to wash.

Washing dishes is an ongoing process that I like to keep up with, but I sometimes fall behind, letting the dishes stack up in the sink. Then, of course, I have more work to do at one time. If I fooled myself into believing that I have washed all the dishes *once and for all,* I would be extremely disappointed and probably pretty angry when they began to accumulate again.

Living with an attitude of self-forgiveness is the same as washing dishes. There will always be more to do, it feels great when everything is clean, and sometimes we fall behind.

What I am describing is nothing more than adopting a realistic view of yourself. In some ways, self-forgiveness is simply a matter of accepting our human imperfections. This is far easier said than done, especially if you have been thoroughly trained to be a negatively arrogant pessimist. But remember: Just because something is difficult doesn't mean that it can't be done.

Conscious Thinking

Our thoughts operate according to the physical principle of *no two objects can occupy your mind at the same time.* Try as you may, you cannot hold more than one conscious thought at a time. When you think you are doing so, what you're actually doing is alternating rapidly between more than one thought.

Say the word "blue," then "pink," then "white," then "blue" again. Say the word "elephant." In the moment that you say the word, your conscious mind will focus entirely there. It will quickly move on, maybe to something like, "What is the point of this silly exercise?" The point is to show you that in any given moment, there is within you *only one conscious thought.* This means that all of your thoughts have to compete for that one space. And this makes that one space a highly valuable commodity.

Responding

Consider the idea of your mind having space for only one conscious thought at a time.

Who chooses how the precious space will be used? What are the thoughts that occupy that space most of the time? What are the various thoughts that compete for the space? What are some thoughts that don't even try?

Ask yourself lots of questions like these.

Responsible Replacement Thoughts

When you are consumed by self-criticism, condemnation, and negativity, there is not much room for the thoughts of your own choosing. The truth is most of us are sloppy thinkers and very poor guardians of that one precious present-time space.

To practice self-forgiveness is to recognize when harmful thoughts occupy your mind and to replace them with new thoughts of your own design and choice. Remember, no two thoughts can occupy your mind at the same time. By persistently pushing the *replacement thought* into your mind, you dislodge the toxic thought. Here are some examples of toxic thoughts and some corresponding replacement thoughts.

My wife is always upset with me, and I don't blame her. I'm a jerk.	I will ask my wife if she is upset with me.
I am getting old, and I am out of shape.	I can choose to stay physically fit and youthful.
I'll never get promoted; I never have good ideas.	I'll start doing more research and look for good, solid new ideas.

In your journal, keep up with some of your more prevalent negative thoughts about yourself, and create some replacement thoughts that are more positive *and more realistic*. Being realistic will help build credibility. For instance, if I am worried about paying my bills this month, which one of the following will be the most reassuring to me?

1. Don't worry, Thom, you are going to win the sweepstakes within the next two weeks.

2. Don't worry, Thom, one of your books will show increased sales this quarter, and that will give you a little financial padding.

3. Thom, you have a full week of clients scheduled, and a couple of speaking engagements where you will have the opportunity to sell some books and tapes.

Can you see that all of these statements are positive, but that the more realistic they are, the more credibility—and therefore reassurance—they have? That doesn't mean that statements one and two are not good thoughts. Perhaps I will keep both of them, but I will make sure that the third, most realistic statement involving taking some action gets to stay on my mind more than the others.

The Freedom to Be Responsible

If you want to choose the thoughts that have the most value for you, or are in your best interest, will that make you a selfish person? Or will it make you a responsible person?

First, we are all selfish people, and we are all responsible people, and there are infinitely more adjectives we could use to characterize ourselves. One mistake we can practice stepping around is all or nothing thinking. It is not nearly as valuable to know if you're a selfish or a responsible person as it is to know if you're acting selfishly or responsibly right now. Let's leave the characterizations for the historians with all that good 20/20 hindsight.

Second, choosing the thoughts that will have the most value for you will not determine one way or the other if you'll be selfish or responsible. What making such a choice will do is to give you even a greater freedom to choose how you will think, and especially how you'll choose to act. When you choose replacement thoughts that will empower you and encourage you, not only will you be aware of more choices, but you'll also be motivated to make those choices.

As long as you leave the decisions to The Should Monster, or to some defeatist part of your thinking, you will, by your own inaction, be limited in your choices. As long as negative, self-critical thoughts and beliefs occupy that central space in your conscious mind and you do nothing about it, you'll have made a choice that will deaden your awareness of your greater expanse of choices.

By choosing replacement thoughts that are supportive, creative, and realistic, you move to the next level of play, like in a video game. The more choices you make, the more authority you claim over your own thought process, the more choices you'll have. Choices beget choices. And choices are freedom.

Can you choose selfishness? You bet you can, and sometimes you will, but even then what is most important is that you accept responsibility for your choices. You must put yourself appropriately in the line of accountability fire.

The way I think of being self-forgiving and realistic is this: I am not *in control* of most of what happens in my life; none of us are. But I am fully *in charge* of my life. That is, *I am the one who, whatever life deals me, will be making the decisions about how to think, and how to act in response.*

The Seven Components of Self-Forgiveness

Once you can see how excessive self-criticism blocks you from being the responsible people you are intended (and want) to be, and you find new motivation for learning to live a life of self-compassion, you need a map, something tangible to show you how to get where you want to go.

My book *The Self-Forgiveness Handbook* was written as just that kind of map. If you work with the principles presented in this chapter and still feel stuck in self-criticism, consider reading that book. For the purposes of this chapter, I will present a summary of The Seven Components of Self-Forgiveness, as they are described in *The Self-Forgiveness Handbook.*

Component One: Acknowledging the Committee

First, you must admit that you are never just one person. The better you can understand that having *multiple opinions and feelings* about matters that are important to you, the less you will feel confused, or even crazy, when you are experiencing what amounts to differing opinions within the so-called singular mind. As far-fetched as it may seem, it can be very helpful to actively imagine that your mind is made up of many committee members sitting around a big conference room table. Identify the various committee members in your mind notice; how each of their communication styles and temperaments differ from one another. Become a curious observer of the workings of your committee. Maybe try keeping the minutes for a meeting or two.

Component Two: Identifying The Should Monster in Charge

We have already discussed The Should Monster. Now, imagine The Should Monster as a member of your committee. Maybe he monopolizes much of the available time and/or interrupts other committee members to impose his point of view. Notice how much a dominating Should Monster can throw the committee off balance. Learn to identify the voice of your Should Monster, and most important, learn to distinguish it from your own thinking. The ultimate goal of this component is to *see yourself in relationship with The Should Monster* and become capable of *disagreeing* with him. (*To The Should Monster: I see you, I hear you, and I disagree with you.*)

Component Three: Understanding the Should Source

You need to know something about how the self-criticism developed in the first place. This usually involves some looking back into what you learned growing up in your family. The purpose of this exploration is primarily to help you to see that whatever the problems you're now facing, you came by them honestly—that there is a perfectly rational way to understand how those problems developed. Component three is not about laying blame on your parents or on anyone else, but it is about discovering how the adults in your life as a child might have fallen short (regardless of their intentions) in meeting their responsibilities. The goal of this component is for you to let go of any attachment you have to blaming yourself for circumstances over which you had no control.

Component Four:
Discovering a Decision Maker

At this point, you'll have hopefully accepted the committee within, practiced identifying and disagreeing with The Should Monster, and begun to let go of much of your self-blame. Next you need to find within yourself a part of you that can learn to stand up to The Should Monster on a regular basis and begin taking charge of your life. A *Decision Maker* is the part that creates and installs the replacement thoughts we discussed earlier in this chapter. A Decision Maker accepts, as its first responsibility, taking care of you. (I'll have much more to say about decision making later in the book.)

Component Five:
Building the Power

As difficult as it is to face your own destructive self-criticism, often the greater challenge is in creating and empowering your new Decision Maker. Initially, The Decision Maker will have no credibility, and it will feel weak or even silly. You must make and maintain a strong commitment to *standing up in the face of The Should Monster* and other negative thinking. Only with the practical application of all that you have learned will you become your own best ally, a powerful and benevolent Decision Maker.

Component Six:
Learning to Succeed

I think the so-called *fear of success* is a thinly veiled version of the *fear of failure*. It's not success that we fear so much as it is the responsibilities and expectations that go with it. We are afraid that we won't be able to handle it, that success will only set us up for a bigger fall. In addition, we have been listening to (and believing) negative interpretations of ourselves for years and years, to the point where

we have well-developed bad habits in our thinking. Learning to succeed involves as much "unlearning" as it does learning. Component
six calls for nothing less than a complete "make-over" of our self-
image. This is where we are challenged—confronted—by the hostage
negotiator: "Put down your negative beliefs, and come out with your
hands above your head."

Component Seven: Practicing, Practicing, Practicing

Perfection is not an option for us as human beings, and as long
as we insist on acting as if it is, we will remain in the painful grasps
of our Should Monsters. The previous six components are useless
without daily practice, and daily practice becomes possible only when
you can learn to accept—and even to value—your human imperfection. The seventh component is an invitation to enjoy life as a constant learning experience. When you accept that invitation, you'll
begin to perceive yourself more accurately—as dynamic and constantly changing. You will stop expecting yourself to become a finished product and realize that as long as you are alive, you're not
finished. Live with self-forgiveness as a daily practice, like exercise,
meditation, or brushing your teeth.

Responding

Consider your strengths and weaknesses in each of The
Seven Components.

Which of The Seven Components presents you with the
greatest challenge?

What are some things you can change right now, based on
The Seven Components?

Empty-Handed

Let's return for a moment to the analogy of the hostage negotiator
speaking through the bullhorn, asking that you put down your
negative beliefs about yourself and come out with your hands held
high. It's a silly little analogy that I began using in my presentations

and workshops mainly because I could usually get a laugh or two out of it.

A few months ago, I was answering questions and listening to comments from an audience I had just addressed, and a woman who had so far remained quiet spoke: "I liked your analogy of the hostage negotiator, not because I could identify with the negotiator, but because I know how vulnerable and defenseless I feel whenever I even think about being without my very familiar negative self-talk. I can see—and feel—myself putting the negative thoughts on the ground, then rising back to my feet slowly, putting my hands high in the air to show them empty, and then I take one step after another, moving with great fear out into the world." The woman closed her eyes and continued, speaking in the present tense. "I am acutely aware that my hands are empty, that I have no weapons, and with my hands in the air, my whole self feels exposed. I suspect that there might be a big target painted on me. And I am aware of a crowd of people all around, watching me as I inch my way from my safe haven out into the dangerous world."

"What awaits you in that dangerous world?" I asked cautiously, not wanting to interrupt her spontaneous visualization.

She took a small breath, and I could see her think for a moment. Then she replied, "Risk. Risk is waiting for me. One risk after another."

Thanks, But No Thanks

That's not a bad definition for life: one risk after another. When you really decide to live your life, you're deciding to walk headlong into the risks that lie ahead of you. Eyes wide open . . . okay, maybe closing them and ducking every once in a while. After all, perfection is not an option, right?

All of the negativity, criticism, and fears that rise from within us are there to tell us to turn back. "Don't risk it," The Should Monster says. "Why do something that you are only going to fail? Go back to your safe little room, and stay there. Believe me," The Should Monster continues, "you won't be hurt if you listen to me. I am stopping you from taking this risk for your own good. Stay right here with me, where you belong."

Read the previous paragraph again. Try speaking the words of The Should Monster aloud. Can you hear The Should Monster as a frightened, negative, and overprotective parent? Ultimately, that's what it is, and when we can see it from that perspective, we can even learn how to forgive The Should Monster.

"I understand that you mean well," you might say to it, "but I am no longer willing to live my life from a place of fear. Even if I need to fall flat on my face now and then, I'm still going to risk living my life rather than listening to you for more and more creative ways to avoid taking risks. I understand now that your intentions have been to protect me from the big wide world, but now I no longer want to be protected. I thank you for all you have done for me, and especially for your good intentions, but as for your offer to continue running my life—thanks, but no thanks."

Responding

Write a personal *Declaration of Independence* from your Should Monster.

PART II

Getting Practice

... both bitterness and true happiness are choices that we make, not conditions that fall on us by fate.

—Dean Koontz
Sole Survivor

4

Self-Esteem

Taking Action and Feeling Better

I have always been fascinated with the concept of time travel. I love the idea that I might travel back in time to change certain events in order to alter the future for the better. And who hasn't wished to go back in time, knowing then what they know now?

There are countless books, movies, and television programs that enthrall us with stories of time travel, but the concept can be more than just fantasy. Victor Frankl, the author of *Man's Search for Meaning*, founded what he called logotherapy, which purports to teach clients/students "to live as if you were living already for the second time and as if you had acted the first time as wrongly as you are about to act now" (1992). Based on Dr. Frankl's important and inspirational work, and on Rod Sterling's "Twilight Zone," I find it extremely helpful to ask myself, *How can I live this day in a way that even if I were later given the opportunity to change it, I wouldn't want to?* This is a simple, playful, and powerful question that helps me to keep my feet planted firmly in the present, with my conscious mind wide awake.

Just as we discovered in chapter 3 that there is space for only one conscious thought at a time, there is also only one *now* in which we can act on that one conscious thought. Of course there is much to be learned and understood about the past—the complexities that have influenced your development through your lifetime, and in the bigger picture, across time from one generation to the next. But you must not become so distracted by that exploration that you forget that *who you are*—and one day, *who you were*—will be determined by what you do with your one conscious thought in your one "*Now*," again and again.

A house is made of its actual physical parts, not the concepts or the potentials of those parts. In the same way, your life is made of your *interactions* with your environment. When the plans call for a responsible life to be built, responsible thoughts will only be useful when they lead to responsible action. My good intentions and my sincere desire for a new house will not build the house.

Defining Positive Self-Esteem

Creating a positive self-esteem requires rigorous honesty and a sincere commitment to "trying on" new thoughts and new behaviors. Remember, the house does not build itself, and thoughts alone do not make the man or woman. "Trying on" new thoughts and behaviors means putting them into action, frequently before you even halfway believe in them. Creating positive self-esteem also requires that you be involved with other human beings who you trust care about you and who you trust to be honest with you. Genuine self-esteem will not thrive in a less than genuine environment.

If you're experiencing low self-esteem and want to feel better about yourself, you must be willing to accept that at least some of your beliefs—specifically beliefs about yourself—are causing problems because they are *inaccurate* and *incomplete.*

I have worked with many clients whose beliefs about themselves were inaccurate. Someone with an inaccurate perception of himself will not initially not perceive himself in the middle range. Instead, thinking in terms of all good or all bad, he places himself consistently in the latter category. A person whose beliefs about himself are incomplete might accurately perceive certain failures (such as lost jobs or problems in relationships) but not take the next essential step into believing that he has the power to change what is happening to him. If you have incomplete beliefs about yourself, a good question to ask is, *What else? What else do I know about myself and this situation? What else can I do that has not yet been done?* If the answer comes back, *Nothing,* then ask the questions again. Always insist on a better than "nothing" answer to the "what else" question.

Positive self-esteem is based on reality: It is the awareness that you are as good as anyone else; that you are not worth less than anyone else; and that you are not worth more than anyone else. Grandiosity and arrogance should not be mistaken for positive self-esteem any more than feelings of worthlessness and shame should be mistaken for true humility. With genuine positive self-esteem, you are grateful for who you are, and given the choice, you wouldn't choose to be someone else. You are in touch with your personal power as it emanates from within you and do not define that power as something to use against others. A positive self-esteem is affected by your circumstances but is not dependent upon those circumstances.

Responding

In what way are your beliefs about yourself inaccurate?

In what way are they incomplete?

Sources of Self-Esteem

We all have sources of self-esteem. We have some amount of self-esteem just like we must have food, water, and air. As children, if self-esteem is not provided, we will eventually find ways on our own to feed the hunger. To one degree or another, because none of us comes from a perfect family, this applies to us all.

We get our self-esteem, just like nutrition, from a variety of sources. Some people take their self-esteem from only one source—work, and the ability to make money. Consequently, their lives are often out of balance, and they probably miss out on many wonderful opportunities, such as the joy of being a parent, spouse, or friend.

Most of us are out of balance in this department. I am much better than I used to be but still have miles to go. (The upside, I like to tell myself, is that there is plenty of room for growth.) My wife and I moved to a small farm about five years ago. She loves and is at peace with animals, and I liked the idea of living in the country because I had never done it before. Since moving to the farm, I have gained at least a couple of new sources of self-esteem: First, I feel wonderful about and with myself when I am doing something as simple as sitting on the ground feeding ducks out of my hand or when I am taking a walk in the woods with our dogs; and second, I take great pride in having learned how to use most of the tools in my toolbox. Compared to my previous urban self, I have become quite a handyman.

These, of course, are very simple changes, but over time these actions have become new sources of self-esteem. It has not taken effort really, other than the effort it took for me to keep showing up—in this case all I had to do was come home at the end of the day. But it did involve risk; I moved from an environment where I had always felt comfortable in, the city, and where I knew what to expect. The payoff for this former workaholic has been an even easier time shifting my mind and body from my work when the work for each day is done. I have learned to look forward to making the transition to various sources of self-esteem throughout a day. And I do feel more balanced than ever before.

Defining your primary sources for self-esteem is a very subjective process. The standard categories are those such as work, primary relationship, relationships with other family members (such as children, siblings, or parents), relationship with friends, quality time alone, hobbies or recreational activities, avocation or service work, and so on. But you might also consider certain personal characteristics as primary self-esteem sources. For instance, I have leaned heavily on being the "class clown" in group situations throughout my adolescence and well into my adult life. A friend of mine has a lifelong history of always being "the smart one." I am currently working with a client whom I believe (it will ultimately be her decision, not mine) will discover that she is overinvested in her image as a "rebel."

The sources of self-esteem do not necessarily have to yield *positive* self-esteem. Many of us subsist primarily on negative sources of self-esteem. Haven't you ever known someone whom you thought seemed to enjoy being miserable, or at least he seemed extremely invested in his misery? Or someone who seemed satisfied only when she was dissatisfied with something? I don't know about you, but I have not only known people like that, I have *been people like that.* Familiar negativity can serve quite will as a nice, heavy security blanket under which we take refuge when we are not sufficiently aware of the positive alternatives.

Responding

Currently, what are your primary sources of self-esteem?

What changes would you like to make in these sources?

Building a Responsible Adult Self-Image: It's Up to You

When I ask myself how I would live this day if it needed to be lived over again, I am choosing to live by *decision* rather than *default*. When we fall into our day-to-day routines, and allow ourselves to become hypnotized by the repetitious thoughts, feelings, and actions, we are living by default—essentially watching our lives go by without taking an active role. We are waiting for our self-image to build itself, and we are being passive participants in our own lives. That doesn't mean that we don't complain *actively* about our lives, but it does mean that we're behaving as if we don't have choices. Complaining isn't an entirely useless activity, but it absolutely must be accompanied by an awareness that we always have choices.

Responding

What is something you tend to complain about without taking action to change? How are you living your life by default rather than decision?

Consider some of your successes: Make a list of situations in which you did take action when you needed to. What can you learn from these successes?

Growing Up

Andrea was thirty-four years old when I first met her. She was a reluctant client, not because she was being pressured to come to therapy, but because for her, walking into my office was an admission of defeat. She had failed to live up to what she considered to be the very minimum expectations of being a responsible adult. She had made the appointment "as a favor" to her boyfriend, Jim. When I asked her what she expected to gain from the appointment, she said, "No offense to you, but I don't expect much."

"What do you imagine Jim expects you might gain by being here?" I asked.

"He and I are very different in many ways," Andrea sort of chuckled. "I think he believes in miracles, especially therapy miracles."

"Do you think he expects this session to be a miracle for you?"

Andrea smiled. "Yes, I do. And it hurts like hell to think I'm going to disappoint him."

The session produced no miracles, but I learned a lot about Andrea that day, and especially about what appeared to be Andrea's downward spiral of a self-fulfilling prophecy of failure. And maybe one little miracle did happen: Andrea decided that she would return for a second session, and we agreed that the next session would be "a favor to herself."

In the weeks to come, Andrea and I would discover not only that she had become a master of self-sabotage, but also that her best technique for bringing herself to an abrupt and complete halt was what she and I eventually called "backwards thinking."

Andrea spoke of her father as if he were a god. Certainly she saw her dad as the epitome of success, and she sought to emulate him from a very early age. One day I asked Andrea what she imagined her dad had been like as a kid, and without the slightest hesitation, she responded, "Oh, Dad was never a kid." We looked at each other, both of us recognizing the odd combination of inaccuracy and certainty in her reflex response. I probably laughed first (I usually do), but soon we were both laughing. It was more a laughter of relief than of humor; we had finally landed upon a place where Andrea could see for herself that just because something felt like the gospel truth didn't make it so. Of course Andrea's dad had been a kid, but in the depth of Andrea's gut that was an impossibility. And soon to follow was this awareness: Just as her dad was the perpetual adult, Andrea perceived herself as the appropriate counterpart—*the perpetual child.*

Elusive Adulthood

What do you remember about your perceptions of your parents when they were forty years old or so? When my mother was forty-four years old, I was fourteen. When I was fourteen, I wanted to be twenty-two because to me, for whatever reasons, that magic age of twenty-two would signify that I was an adult. Not an adult like my mother and father, but an adult that was young, alive, and free. I thought of my parents in different terms. In fact, I thought of them not as "adults," but as "old."

As I tap this out on the computer screen, I will be forty-four years old in one month and two days. And when I think about it, I am nothing like the image I had of my mother when I was fourteen. I may make a little more noise as I drag myself out of bed in the mornings (audible groans as well as structural pops and cracks), but I'm not *old*. And neither was my mother when she was my age. I guess Einstein said it best: Everybody has relatives.

By the time I turned twenty-two, I had forgotten about what I had thought it would mean to be twenty-two. After all, I had already celebrated my "official adult birthday" at twenty-one, and I had spent some time sweating the military draft lottery after my eighteenth birthday. Being an adult was not looking so attractive by the time I arrived. I spent the next decade doing my very best to avoid becoming an adult.

Andrea, on the other hand, had spent most of her life (including much of her childhood) trying to be an adult, someone like her father—more to the point, someone her father would recognize and value. As children, neither Andrea nor I had accurate perceptions of our parents as human beings, plain ole people involved in the same experience of birth, growth, life, and death that we all are. But Andrea still held onto her childhood perception of her father, and necessarily, her childhood perception of herself. We had our work cut out for us. We decided that nothing less than "crowbar therapy" was called for. Andrea and I were going to find a way to pry her grip from the old beliefs and perceptions that were at the very heart of her faulty and inaccurate self-image.

Responding

Do you have old, ineffective beliefs that are so ingrained in your thinking that you could use some "crowbar therapy"?

Make a list of those beliefs, and practice changing just one belief each week. Even if your negative beliefs seem to persist, just becoming aware of them begins the process of change.

Learning from Your Experience

Andrea had devoted her life to seeking adult status, and yet when we looked closer, she had *no*—as in zero, zip, nada—adult self-image. None. Her self-image had been built from failed attempts to be what she was not—a child trying to be an adult, a little girl trying to be a woman. With her father busy being the epitome of success, there had been no time to celebrate Andrea's arrival on the planet or to share with her the joys of being a child. If Andrea was going to be with her father, her unconscious mind reasoned, she would have to go to where her father was, because her father was certainly not coming for her.

When a child's predominant experience is frustration (which is the guaranteed result when we seek the impossible), she will build a self-image based on those experiences. Andrea literally learned to be repeatedly frustrated and to define herself accordingly. A negative self-image is better than no self-image—everyone needs someplace to hang his hat—and Andrea was smart; she learned quickly and thoroughly.

I asked Andrea for her definition of an adult. "My father, that's what immediately comes to mind," she said, "but that doesn't really answer your question."

I asked her again.

She thought hard, or at least she wrinkled her brow. "An adult is someone who . . . has a job? No, someone who wears a tie? No, has a family? No, gets along with other adults? No, it's more than all that." Andrea was noticeably frustrated, a very familiar experience for her.

I asked her, "How does it feel to be so frustrated right now?"

Again, her response was quick: "Normal," she said.

So What Is an Adult?

Try this: Write the word "adult" at the top of a page in your journal. Then as quickly as you can scribble, write any and all of the words that come to your mind when you think of this one little word. Or just sit back, close your eyes, and repeat the word over and over, like a mantra. As you meditate in this way on the word "adult," become an observer of yourself. Notice everything. What do you feel physically? How do you feel emotionally? What thoughts or images come into your mind? When you have done this for a minute or so, open your eyes and write about your experience in your journal.

I have used these exercises in various forms through the years with clients who have low self-esteem. Although everyone's response is unique, there are some interesting commonalties that I have noticed. With these clients, the word "adult" has tended to evoke feelings of fear, shame, or inadequacy. Many have reported feeling physically constricted, sometimes from the inside, like a tightness in the chest, clenching of the jaw, or their hands forming fists in response to the tension. Several people have reported a feeling of being held back, or held down, as if there were some kind of pressure pushing on them from the outside. Most often, this has been an experience of feeling pressure pushing down on the shoulders, accompanied by an overall sense of feeling "weighted down."

When these clients have free-associated to the words "responsible adult" on paper, here are some of the words that have appeared:

- Strong
- Important
- Disciplined
- Well groomed
- Responsible
- Parental
- Wise
- Experienced
- Organized
- Brave
- Insightful
- Provider

These are extremely positive, powerful words. These are words that we would all like to be applicable to ourselves. So what's the problem?

Unrealistic Expectations

The problem is *expectations*—unrealistic expectations. The words that make the list aren't the problem; the problem is what's missing from the list. Where are words like *imperfect, insecure, self-compassionate, flexible, respectful, human?*

The discussions that often follow this exercise when I use it in my workshops have shown me that our unrealistic expectations of what it means to be an adult are a big obstacle between being an adult, chronologically, and having an *adult self-image*. Think about it. If we create an image of an "adult" version of ourselves that requires that we live up to all of the adjectives in the list above, doesn't it make sense that we're going to seriously consider running in the other direction?

When Andrea set her sights on growing into the image of her father, she was doomed. She was doomed not because it was impossible to succeed in the ways her father had, but because Andrea's image of her father was a fantasy, a greatly exaggerated—in many ways inaccurate—two-dimensional caricature based loosely on her father. When parents don't actively teach us about age-appropiate responsibility as we are growing up, we will create our own curriculum. Andrea did, and in doing so she inadvertently established the *Andrea School of Guaranteed Frustration.*

Outwardly, Andrea was doing fine. She was an account executive for a medium-size advertising firm. She was good at her job, even enjoyed it most of the time, but she wasn't obsessed with her work. She had time for her relationship with Jim and for her friendships with other women. She exercised regularly—racquetball three days a week, running, or walking with Jim whenever they got the chance. I was glad that she hadn't come to me for help balancing her life, because as far as I could tell, she definitely had me beat in that category.

At first, what I called balance, Andrea called laziness. After all, her primary role model was so busy "succeeding" that he hadn't had the time for relationships or for attending to his physical health. He was all about "taking care of business." In fact, Andrea and I decided in one of our sessions that that was probably her father's definition of being an adult—*taking care of business, and nothing but business.* After that session, Andrea began to see how narrow and relentlessly demanding her own definition of being an adult was. And she began to see her father in a new light.

How to Build Your New Self-Image

When I want to refurnish my living room, I will have to make room for whatever new furnishings I will choose. Sometimes that will mean repositioning some of the old, and sometimes that will mean getting rid of it. Either way, since the law of physics states that no two objects can occupy the same space at the same time and a law of home decorating states that a crowded room just won't do, I will have to deal with what is in my living room *now* if I am serious about refurnishing it.

And that is exactly what Andrea had done with her therapy. She had taken an inventory of her current furnishings—expectations, beliefs, interpretations of the world around her—and most of what she found there had been what her father had given her and, more important, what she had accepted automatically, unaware at the time that she had choices. In a sense, the decor of Andrea's psyche had been laid out while she slept. And like so many of us, she just assumed the place came furnished.

Andrea stopped trying to be like her father and began considering the possibility that she could be who she decided to be. For Andrea, and for any of us, this time when we are able to let go of something old, something useless to us, or even destructive to us, can be confusing. When you let go of the old before you know what you will put in its place (like it or not, this seems to be the rule), you will at least feel off balance and at most, scared silly.

We all have attachment to the familiar. The word "familiar" implies predictability if not certainty. It is refuge from the universal fear of the great unknown. With your old furnishings, your self-image by default, you at least know where you stand; you have a definite sense of self, even if the result is self-esteem that leaves much to be desired.

Responding

What parts of your self-image do you think you may be attached to because they are familiar and therefore feel safer than the great unknown?

Reality Check: Looking at Your Strengths

Self-image is the picture (inside and out) that you have of yourself, but there is more to it than that. Just as there must be contrast between object and background for us to visually perceive something, self-image reveals itself in contrast to what—and who—we believe we are *supposed* to be. Therefore there is no such thing as being aware of our self-image without being aware of our self-esteem. Self-esteem, in its simplest form, is what we feel when we experience that contrast, that difference between how we *perceive* ourselves and what we believe we are *supposed* to be.

At the risk of pushing a metaphor too far, I became a home decorating consultant to Andrea, showing her new options and helping her to select what would suit her best.

Getting Help

As we began to structure Andrea's new self-image, I suggested an exercise that I suggest with many of my clients, workshop participants, and now my readers: Ask a few people whom you trust will be honest with you to help you out by writing a short paragraph or a list of characteristics describing how they perceive you. Frightening idea, isn't it? Tell your friends that there is no way to do this wrong, and I recommend that you not give them much more, if any, instruction than what I have described above. The more open the assignment remains, the more interesting the responses.

Obviously this is an emotionally risky experiment, so be careful not to set yourself up by asking people to participate who may not be supportive to the cause. On several occasions, before I learned to add this caution, clients would ask family members to offer their descriptions, and the family members—being caught in the same dysfunctional dynamic as my client—would only reinforce my client's old self-image and resulting low self-esteem. This is not to say that you would not want to include family members in this exercise; just be careful that you only ask people (family or not) who you know support your self-exploration.

Andrea was surprised by the results of her poll. I wasn't surprised. Her friends and family (she did include one brother with whom she was close) described Andrea accurately: *friendly, considerate, moody, creative, funny, controlling, a bit nervous,* and *energetic.* Interestingly, although some of her friends described characteristics that could be perceived in the workplace, none of them listed any description or characteristic that was strictly work related. Unlike Andrea, they saw her for who she was; their view was not obstructed by the internal "father" expectations that had so completely cut Andrea off from herself.

I remember another client, Carl, whose patterns of self-sabotage did not stop with emotional dissatisfaction, but extended into his physical environment. Carl was obviously intelligent but seemed to be always out of gas. The only time Carl would predictably "come alive," displaying considerable energy, was when he was describing to someone else precisely how messed up (he used other words) he was. Like Andrea, Carl's self-esteem was low; he didn't measure up to what he thought he *should* be. Unlike Andrea, when Carl invited his friends to offer their perceptions, he discovered quite a bit of agreement between his self-image and how his friends perceived him. But there was one glaring difference: Carl's friends described him as falling short of what and who he *could* be, instead of *should* be. In fact, I was so interested in this honest feedback that I asked Carl if we could have a couple of his friends join us for one of our sessions. He agreed, and what I learned that day—and Carl began to learn—was how far below his potential he was performing in life. Carl had taken refuge in his failures. By demonstrating again and again that he was not up to this or that task, he kept the expectations of others at bay. Or at least he thought he did—but his good friends were not fooled. They knew Carl well and knew he was smart, funny, and creative.

Andrea was challenged to recognize that she perceived herself inaccurately, as a result of an extremely narrow and biased measuring stick and the absence of someone to teach her how to recognize and celebrate her successes. Carl eventually recognized that he had actively played out his negative self-image, that he could, in fact, create a new, positive self-image, but that a major part of doing so would be to let go of his "security blanket" of failure and actively work to demonstrate his competence.

Hard Work—It's Not So Bad

Do you want positive self-esteem? Of course you do. The better, more productive question to ask yourself is this: *Am I willing to do what it takes to have positive self-esteem?*

At first, the answer to this question seems obvious, but if you've tackled this project you know that it's a little trickier than it looks on the surface. To be willing to "do what it takes" means being willing to identify old beliefs and expectations that have contributed to your negative feelings. That alone can be difficult and painful (why else would we spend so much time, energy, and money trying to avoid these awarenesses?), but the next requirement is even harder. Once we identify them as the culprits that they are, we must make the choice to stop believing these negative, erroneous things about ourselves. And that is a choice that takes a tremendous effort, and a persistent effort. It's not a choice we make one time; we make this choice over and over and over again, for as long as it takes to tip the scale in our favor. For many, I believe that this work is as difficult and as tedious as working to become left handed when I am naturally right handed.

Of course, it's hard work. In renovating our self-image and improving our self-esteem, we are rewiring years and years of programming, most of which was installed before we even knew how to make a choice.

Taking Responsibility for Your Self-Esteem

This may sound like chicken-or-the-egg reasoning, but here goes: Since positive self-esteem is a necessary component of accepting full responsibility for yourself, you must accept the responsibility to create and maintain (by imperfect human standards, of course) positive self-esteem. *Who's on first? What? No, what's on second?*

Accepting this responsibility doesn't mean that you accept all of the blame for everything that happens to you in your life. To turn this into a matter of blame is a serious and common problem with this component. When you interpret this mistakenly as the need to accept responsibility for other people in your life—and their actions—you cannot succeed in creating positive self-esteem. In fact, you can never have positive self-esteem when you're expecting the impossible of yourself; and taking on responsibility or blame for another person's decisions and actions puts you in that impossible circumstance. Interestingly, many of us have discovered that attempting to take on responsibility for others in our lives has actually been a clever way to avoid some responsibilities of our own.

Your Turn

The measure of your self-esteem is the degree of comfort you have in your own company. You need to ask, "How do I feel about spending a full day with myself, just me and me, without a long list of things to do?" I suggest that you actually schedule a day with yourself. Better yet, schedule one day a month with yourself. If that seems too much to ask, have a talk with yourself and the two of you come up with an alternate plan to help you practice being in your own company. After all, it is your responsibility.

5

Congruence

Acting Out Your Personal Values

What matters most to you? What are the regrets you definitely *don't* want to have when you reflect on your life from your deathbed? What are the memories you definitely *do* want to have as you look back? Are you living this very day of your life in a way that is congruent with your answers to these three questions?

> *Well, no, not exactly. But I have a desk full of late projects that I have to complete to get even just a little breathing room.*

or

> *I need to make more of an effort to stay in touch with friends, people who really matter to me. And I plan to do a better job of that beginning this very minute.*

or

> *I'm not even sure what my answers to the first two questions are. For years now I have just been taking life as it comes, dealing only with whatever the next circumstance is. I used to think about what in life mattered most to me, but now I couldn't say for sure.*

or

I think I know what matters most to me, and I thought I was doing a pretty good job living a life that is consistent with my beliefs . . . but now that you mention it, I haven't stopped to think about it in quite a while.

What matters most to you? What are the regrets you definitely don't want to have when you reflect on your life from your death-bed? What kind of memories do you want to have as you look back? You need to ask yourself questions like these—and be able to answer them—on a regular basis. It should be like checking the oil in your car.

We all have our own unique set of values. It is important that you explore and define your value system so that you can act in congruence with your values on a daily basis. There are three parts to the concept of congruency: (1) becoming conscious of your personal value systems, (2) knowing that once our eyes are open, value systems are built, revised, and maintained according to our choices, and (3) to the very best of our imperfect ability, we act according to our expressed value systems.

Reminding yourself that you are working with a time limit, whether you like it or not, can become the impetus for you to take an important and serious look at how you're living your life. The reality of inevitable death staring you square in the face can be a life-saving awareness if it's put to good use. It can inspire you to examine your personal value system and the congruence of your behavior with your value system.

Far too many of us live significant parts of our lives by default, simply falling into the next circumstance, relationship, or job because that is where the path leads. We forget to ask the question—or maybe no one ever taught us to ask it—*Wait, I can choose which path to take according to where I want it to lead me.*

Envisioning Your Life: Choosing Your Path

If you and I decide to take a walk in the woods and we walk into those woods at a point where a narrow but distinct dirt path begins, probably without either one of us giving it much thought, we will follow the path. We may become engrossed in conversation, not paying attention to exactly where we are going, allowing the path to guide our direction. It is as if we put our bodies on autopilot. We're not unconscious; we are just otherwise engaged, distracted. When we come to a fork in the path, we will probably stop for a moment and discuss casually which way to go, deciding eventually to take which-ever route looks pleasant enough. Then, we're back on autopilot until the next obvious choice (fork in the path) presents itself.

That's not such a bad way for two friends to take a walk and enjoy each other's company. But many of us live our lives on the same kind of autopilot, following a path that has been worn naturally or perhaps purposely made by other people. There's nothing wrong with walking the paths of those who have gone before us; that's not the problem. The problem is that far too often, we are walking these paths and have never made a conscious decision to do so. The prob-lem is the absence of decision.

Maybe you are on a path your mother or father started you on many years ago. Or maybe you are on a path you chose many years ago, specifically to rebel against your parents. Maybe you don't even know how you got on your present path. Maybe you know exactly why you are on this particular path, but you're unaware that you can change your mind and choose another path if you want.

Responding

Describe the path you are walking. Have you walked other paths in the past? Do you have plans to change paths in the future? Do you feel free to venture off the path if you want to?

What relationship is there between your current path and what matters most to you?

Tapping into Your Inner Parent

In the midst of the codependency-recovery movement in the mid-1980s, Robert Subby, author of *Lost in the Shuffle*, spoke to the issue of personal responsibility in a clever and succinct way. He said, "As children we are victims, as adults we are volunteers." I was for-tunate enough to hear Mr. Subby speak on a number of occasions, and each time he emphasized his belief that people who grew up in dysfunctional environments must not hold themselves responsible for the shortcomings of their parents and other childhood caregivers, but he cautioned the same people not to let themselves off the hook of responsibility as adults (1987).

I eventually translated this bit of wisdom into a seminar entitled *Discovering the Parent Within*. People were drawn to that seminar because it offered a way to move beyond the pain, discomfort, or confusion of their childhood experiences and into a tangible sense of personal responsibility. The goal of this seminar was for participants to leave with renewed hope that they could be in charge of their own lives. My favorite way to begin the opening lecture was by saying, "The only reason to discover the child within is so that we can create a job description for the parent within."

As an adult you are walking the path you're on, either by *decision* or by *default*. Either way, you have the right and the ability to change course. That doesn't mean that taking the initiative to live proactively is easy; it may be the hardest work you will ever do. But, as I remind my clients—and myself—frequently: Just because something is difficult doesn't mean that it can't be done.

Remembering Your Dreams

Are you living the life that you choose to live? Are you living more by default or by decision? These questions, along with the questions throughout this chapter and book, are powerful tools to help you take stock of who you are, where you are, and precisely how congruent your life is with your value system.

During a weekend retreat that I held a couple of years ago, the group of about eighteen or twenty of us were involved in an interesting discussion when someone asked, "What would you be doing with your time if you were guaranteed financial abundance for the rest of your life, without having to work for it?" As soon as the question was asked I glanced around the room, remembering what I could about the participants' financial circumstances.

I knew very little about most of these people's day-to-day lives, even though I'd already spent most of the weekend with them and was privy to very intimate details of their inner lives. My quick scan of the group told me that we were a group with a broad spectrum of socio-economic status. One young woman, Bev, in her early thirties, was living in a small apartment with almost no furniture. She had been released from a three-year prison stay about a year before and had been in therapy with me since shortly after her release. Bev had no money to speak of; she worked as a receptionist at an alcohol and drug rehabilitation program, probably making minimum wage.

Hal was a forty-five-year-old man, sitting directly across the room from Bev. Hal was living the circumstance posed by the question. He would never have to work a day in his life. He had more money than he would ever come close to spending in two lifetimes. I don't think anyone else in the group knew just how financially secure Hal was.

The rest of us fell somewhere between the two, most of us closer to Bev's end of the scale. The question of how we would choose to spend our time if we didn't have to work for a living soon led to participants revealing their dreams to the group. The question became, "What have you always wanted to do?"

The group included a woman whose ambition to dance professionally was stopped when she was badly injured in a car accident, a would-be stand-up comedian, a few songwriters and musicians who were in the throes of pursuing their dreams (I live and work in Nashville after all), and several people who talked about wanting to work for themselves rather than hold traditional jobs. As I listened, I thought of the old Billy Joel song, "Piano Man," in which he describes the patrons of a bar in terms of their lost dreams. There is Paul, "the real-estate novelist," and the bartender who knows that he could be a movie star if he "could just get out of this place." I thought about how losing touch with our dreams is such a universal experience. The world we live in is so full of distractions; it's like an obstacle course for dreamers.

I was interested to learn that Bev's priority was pursuing work that was meaningful for her, something that would draw out her strengths from her experiences. Hal, on the other hand, worried about money a lot. It was one more validation for me that we don't pay much attention to our *outer lives*. We are much more the products of our *inner lives*. And which one of these people at two economic extremes was more in touch with his or her dream and living more in line with that dream? You guessed it: Bev. She seemed well on her way to becoming an excellent and talented counselor. She was still uncertain and insecure to see that future for herself, but she knew she felt passionate about working with people, especially the adolescents she came in contact with at her job.

Hal described himself in terms of his fears and disconnection from any sense of purpose in his life. He told the group that he wasn't sure that he had ever had a dream for himself—probably, he said, because "I grew up with a full set of instructions about *who I would be, how I would act,* and even *who I would love.*" Borrowing a succinct phrase from Bev's earlier description of life in prison, Hal looked straight across the room to Bev and said, "Now that I think about it, it really sucked." We all laughed.

Responding

What are your dreams? Is there something you have always wanted to do?

What are the distractions in your life that make it difficult for you to maintain contact with what you really want to be doing?

Wake-Up Calls

Sometimes we get slapped with the reality of our ultimate limitations, and then we begin to remember what matters most to us. It is certainly not unusual to hear of people talking about how a close encounter with death changed their outlook on life entirely. These people don't describe their lives as having been changed; they describe *themselves* as having been changed.

And we don't have to have a dramatic near-death experience to identify with this kind of fundamental change of being. People will frequently report feeling much more in touch with the value of their lives after a friend or relative has died. In fact, most of us will come and go from such awareness throughout the course of our lives. Having narrowly escaped a potentially fatal accident or hearing that an acquaintance who was only forty-four years old dropped dead of a heart attack last Wednesday, we may come to an abrupt halt. We think about the experience we have just had or the news we have just heard, and we resolve to pay more attention to what in life is really important and not to "sweat the small stuff" anymore. Immediately our wives and husbands and children and friends reap the benefits. We come home from work early to play with the kids. We surprise our spouses with a romantic weekend in the mountains or on the beach. We decide to put down a professional journal for a change and begin to read—or even to write—that novel we have been putting off until "there was time." It's wonderful.

Then time passes; a couple of weeks, or maybe a month. We're back to the same old grind. The evidence of our amazing existential revelation has faded. We still love our families and friends, and we're as good to them as we have been in the past. However, all that life-affirming, in-the-moment ecstacy is gone.

It is just like getting a traffic ticket. I get a ticket for speeding today. Beginning immediately, I pay more attention to my driving speed—especially along the stretch of road where the police pulled me over. For a couple of days, you could even say I am a careful and conscientious driver. Only two or three days, and I am back to speeding along the roadways. I haven't made a decision to return to speeding; in fact, the opposite has happened. I lost touch with my decision to not speed.

If any of this sounds familiar, welcome to the human race—the memory-challenged, easily-distracted human race.

Responding

Remember a time or two in your life when something happened to wake you up to what you consider to be most important in your life.

Did you make decisions in response to reality's confrontation? Have you remained true to your decision(s)?

Remembering to Pay Attention

Try this little exercise. Sit comfortably wherever you are right now, straighten your spine, and a take a deep, relaxing breath. Next, practice this simple breath-counting meditation. Counting *one* as you inhale a full deep breath and *two* as you let go of that breath, exhaling completely, then *three* with the next inhale, *four* with the exhale, *five,* the next inhale—do this exercise, counting your breaths up to *ten,* then starting over. If you lose your place, if your mind wanders or you become distracted from the count, start over at *one.* Do this exercise now, before reading further.

What happened? How many times did you count your breaths straight through to *ten* and then start over? If you are among the great majority, you will have discovered it to be virtually impossible to get straight through to *ten*—without cheating, that is. Our minds wander, the task being in this case, a simple breath count to *ten.*

This is what we're given to work with, our amazing human attention span. No wonder I never seem to remember all of the phone calls I am supposed to make. I once heard someone say that as human beings we all have the disease of forgetfulness and that one of our primary challenges in our lives is *remembering* and *reminding each other*. That is, we must accept the chronic nature of our "forgetting disease" and in response make specific plans for being regularly reminded to remember. We must find ways to remind ourselves (tying strings around our fingers?), we must become willing and available to be reminded by others, and we must do our part to become respectful reminders for our fellow memory-impaired human beings. Otherwise, it's just too easy to drift back into living by default.

Making Proactive Decisions: Don't Be a Victim

Every day we must decide to be either *passive* or *proactive* in our lives. To remain passive—living by default—is to reject our personal power. Whether we are giving that power away to others (to a spouse, a boss, or society in general) or simply refusing to acknowledge and use it ourselves, the result is the same: *victimization*.

A victim is someone who believes that how he is doing and feeling is determined more by his outside circumstances than by how he responds to those circumstances. Someone who is a proactive participant in his life, on the other hand, knows that although he isn't usually in charge of which cards will be dealt him, his well-being depends not on those cards—or his circumstances—but on his ability to respond to those cards. The proactive participant believes in his *ability to respond*, otherwise known as *responsibility*.

Deciding to Be a Decision Maker

Sometimes it seems like there are as many different ways to define psychotherapy as there are clients. The process of psychotherapy is so personal and subjective. There are, however, common threads that run through all of my work with clients, workshop participants, and readers. One of those commonalities is the sense that no matter who I'm talking with and no matter what we're talking about, *I am there to help uncover that person's ability and willingness to accept full responsibility for making his or her own decisions.*

We are all in a learning process, moving away from perceptions of ourselves as victims and toward new, more useful, and more accurate perceptions of ourselves as decision makers, in charge of our own lives. And remember, being *in charge* doesn't mean that we delude ourselves into believing we are *in control*. To the contrary, as long as we fight to hold onto the perception of ourselves as in control, or even potentially in control, we will continue to perceive ourselves as at the mercy of our circumstances.

Am I being a victim, or am I being a Decision Maker? This question, though useful, can be improved upon. Because there are always several members of that committee at work in our consciousness, and since unanimous opinions from the committee are rare (or nonexistent), the better questions are, *In what ways am I either being—or being tempted to be—a victim in this situation? In what ways am I being a proactive Decision Maker?* Asking both questions will not only give us more information, it will also help us to remain grounded in the reality that at any given time, any one of us is a collection of thoughts and feelings that are seldom in total agreement.

We need to remember, and remind each other, that being in charge of our lives means gathering enough information to make intelligent choices, then making those choices and moving on to the next challenge. To be fully responsible, we must make those choices based on both the external information available to us and our own personal value systems. Being in charge requires that through our decision making, we build and maintain that personal value system; and acting responsibly means that we put that value system to work in our actions.

When we are acting as proactive Decision Makers, we know that in most circumstances it is unrealistic to wait for absolute certainty before making our choices. To engage in that waiting game is familiar to many of us and is an excellent way to avoid risks and to remain stuck. There is no decision making without risk, just as there is no learning without mistakes. *Being a Decision Maker is choosing to be involved in a life-long process of developing practical intelligence and good judgment, the kind of good sense we need to face life's daily pop-tests.*

Responding

What do you know about yourself as a victim? What is your style of victimization? In what ways is remaining a victim easier or more comfortable to you?

What do you know about yourself as a Decision Maker? What is your Decision Maker's relationship to your victim-self?

What important decisions are you facing now in your life? How can you be proactive about these decisions?

Behavioral Decisions

Becoming a Decision Maker is important work, but if we stop there, it is only a matter of time until we slide back into our old familiar patterns of thinking and acting. This is similar to the reason we speed again after we get the traffic ticket. We make a decision, and then we stop there, either believing that the decision will be enough to instigate and maintain long-term change or giving it little or no thought one way or the other.

If I'm married to a woman and I say that I love her, what will that tell you about me as a husband? Not much, right? Although expressing love verbally is a behavior, and a pretty important behavior in many instances, it is not possible to tell what the expression means, or if it means anything. The expression of love requires behavioral backup. To form an opinion about whether or not I genuinely love my wife, you would look for *congruence*.

Consider the congruence or lack of congruence in the following:

I love my wife.	I forget her birthday.
I love my wife.	I ask her to go out to dinner with me on Friday night.
I love my wife.	I am having an affair with another woman.
I love my wife.	I don't pay much attention to her or our relationship because I am busy with my work. I've been planning to change that for years.
I love my wife.	I listen to her tell me about her fears and dissatisfactions about our relationship.

Can you detect the varying degrees of congruence and incongruence? Forgetting a birthday is not as incongruent with my expressed love as is having an affair. Taking my wife to dinner on a Friday night is not as much a behavioral expression of love as is listening to her fears and dissatisfactions about our relationship. If a picture is worth a thousand words, a behavior is worth at least fifty thousand.

Consider these examples:

A little boy grows up without his father ever saying "I love you" to him. The little boy is a grown man now and cannot remember his father ever touching him with affection—not so much as an awkward hug. The little boy's mother, however, always made it a point to tell him that his father loved him very much, sometimes offering excuses for her husband like "He had a hard day" and "He just doesn't know how to show his love."

A controlling man lives with his girlfriend who is about ten years his junior. He frequently tells her he loves her and brings her gifts regularly. He says he wants her to know how special she is to him. When they go out socially, however, he is extremely critical of his girlfriend—including how she dresses, how much makeup she wears, how she acts when talking with other men. On the occasions that she has objected to his constant critiques, he has screamed at her, sometimes calling her hurtful names. By morning, he will usually apologize, but not without adding that "she has to admit" that she wasn't totally innocent in starting the argument. That evening, he will bring her a "thoughtful" gift.

Each night before a couple goes to sleep, they kiss and say "I love you" to one another. They have breakfast together almost every morning. Other than those two times of contact, they have very separate lives, each of them involved in his or her own work and his or her own extracurricular interests.

Again, can you detect the varying degrees of incongruence in these examples? I cannot say with any certainty what any of these people in the situations actually feel. Maybe the father did feel love for the little boy; maybe the man does want his girlfriend to know that she is special; and maybe the couple going their separate ways really do love each other. But no matter what any of them feel, *their behaviors fail to adequately express a congruent message.*

Unfortunately, most of us have learned to one degree or another to keep listening to *the words*, even when the congruent behavior does not follow. We have even been taught, explicitly or by example, to distrust our own perceptions and instead to believe someone else's words (such as, "You know your father loves you. Why do you make it so hard for him to show it?").

When something expressed verbally is not accompanied by congruent behavior, you have every right to question the sincerity of what is being said. When the congruence of your own words and behaviors is called into question, you have the responsibility to look honestly and seriously into the problem until it is resolved. In other words, you must always be ready to confront yourself, demanding that you put your actions where your mouth is.

Confronting Yourself and Your Actions

Earlier in my career, I probably spent most of my time as a psychotherapist helping people to see all that they were *not* responsible for. The codependency-recovery movement was at its height. My emphasis, like many of my colleagues, was on exploring my client's *family-of-origin issues.* I wanted to help my clients see that they were not responsible for what their parents had said or done—that those same parents had often passed on erroneous and negative (sometimes dangerous) belief systems and modeled dysfunctional relationship dynamics that would inevitably be reenacted by their children, now my clients.

I still believe that these are important lessons to learn. It is a mistake to underestimate the impact that our childhood experiences have had on our adult lives. I continue to emphasize that we need to be very careful not to assume responsibility for someone else's choices—especially when the "someone else's" were adults and we were children. And I believe that understanding *what we learned* and *how we learned* in our families of origin is a powerful and necessary component of freeing ourselves from problems with excessive self-criticism and self-condemnation. I now spend considerably more time helping my clients to identify what they *are* responsible for rather than what they are not. My shift in focus is due in part to my personal growth toward accepting responsibility and in part to my professional experience that has consistently validated that focusing on accepting responsibility is a powerful and efficient way to bring about desired changes.

I teach people how to confront themselves with their incongruities. Many of us think that we know how to confront ourselves, but in fact what we call confrontation is often unmitigated attack and condemnation. We know how to kick ourselves around; we know how to insult and demean ourselves; but most of us have never learned how to confront ourselves effectively.

Effective confrontation—of yourself as well as others—is both respectful and compassionate. Confrontation is really nothing more than placing the truth front and center, making it as difficult as possible to avoid seeing that truth. But beware of tendencies toward assaulting yourself with excessive self-criticism in the name of healthy confrontation. This can happen easily considering the distorted, negative version of "the truth" that many of us have come to accept.

There is a big difference between recognizing your mistakes and shortcomings in order to support the big *I-Told-You-So-Within* (*I told you that you couldn't do it. You shouldn't have even tried*) and confronting the same mistakes and shortcomings to improve yourself. Don't waste your regrets; learn the lessons.

Responding

What does the *I-Told-You-So-Within* like to say when it gets the opportunity? *I told you that you would fail? I told you that you don't fit in? I told you that nobody likes you?*

Write some examples of healthy self-confrontations. For example, *I can do better than that; I will increase my practice time beginning right now. Even when my intention is good, I can still be pretty controlling—I'm going to ask some friends to help me recognize when that is happening.*

6

Motivation

Working toward Change

If you want your car to go, you are going to need fuel. And if you plan on taking responsibility for yourself, you are going to need motivation. Motivation can be defined as feelings of *dissatisfaction* combined with a *desire to make a change,* plus belief that change is *possible.* In other words, you have to want it (desire), and you have to believe that it is possible (hope).

Desire + Hope = Motivation

Anthony Robbins, in his book *Awaken the Giant Within,* tells us that we are not unlike our animal cousins in that we are motivated in just two ways: (1) efforts to avoid pain, and (2) efforts to seek pleasure (1991). To become fully self-responsible, you must become proficient in identifying and benefiting from both kinds of motivation, and you must learn how they work together to produce change.

Negative Motivation

Consider the formula for motivation in terms of *avoiding pain.* When we are motivated by our desire to avoid discomfort or pain, the object of our efforts is a *negative;* that is, our focus is on *not* experiencing something. We aren't concerned with what the alternative is; all we care about is that there *is* an alternative to feeling our pain. This is similar to living by default in that we are not acting proactively. We may not even have any idea what we want to experience instead of the pain from which we are retreating.

I worked with a man named Mitchell in individual and in group psychotherapy for a couple of years. He insisted on defining himself by his past problems rather than his accomplishments. That is, Mitchell's negative past behaviors dominated his perception of himself; his main focus was on who he did *not* want to be rather than who he *did* want to be. Mitchell's personal identity was a collection of negative and toxic behaviors and thinking patterns that he no longer engaged in.

Mitchell thought of himself as a man who *used* to drink excessively, who *used* to be unfaithful to his wife, and who *used* to spend money recklessly. After encountering some very tough, hurtful consequences for his toxic behaviors, he had reached out for help from friends and eventually began attending twelve-step support groups. There was no denying that he had made a miraculous turnaround; he had every right to feel good about what he had accomplished by intervening so drastically in his out-of-control behaviors. What concerned me was Mitchell's almost total inability to speak of himself in positive terms. From his point of view he was the same out-of-control man he had been previously, except he was not acting out those toxic behaviors.

I have worked with addictive behaviors for much of my career, and I know that as people begin recovery from these problems (alcohol, drugs, sex, spending, gambling, food, and so on) it is important that they see themselves—even begin to define themselves—as someone who *used* to engage in certain behaviors but no longer do so. This is where the rebuilding of self-esteem begins. The newly recovering addict is encouraged to embrace the ability to choose *not* to act out the old behaviors and to identify with others who have overcome similar problems. In brief, the first step toward positive self-esteem is to make the move from an identity of "out-of-control addict" to an identity of "recovering addict."

We don't have to be diagnosed as addicts to understand the importance of having the ability to intervene in behaviors that are somehow damaging or even dangerous to ourselves or to those who love us and depend on us. The beginning step to change is often finding the ability to interrupt and discontinue one or more of these behaviors. At those times, we are usually responding to negative consequences encountered as a direct result of our less-than-healthy behaviors. We are being fueled by *negative motivation*.

When Negative Is Positive

Don't let the term mislead you. Negative motivation can be a useful, necessary, even positive thing. Negative motivation simply means that we are motivated to change in order to avoid previously experienced or potentially negative consequences. The alcoholic or addicted gambler, for instance, might begin recovery in order to save his marriage or to keep his job. The woman who has bulimia might begin therapy because she has begun to develop health problems caused by poor nutrition.

Working in the addiction recovery field for so many years, I began to think of the word "recovery" as having two distinct applications. First, you must *recover* from whatever is toxic in your life. Second, you are then in a position *to recover* (meaning reconnect, regain, or rediscover) who you really are.

For the substance abusers I work with, "recovery from" obviously means abstinence from mood-altering chemicals. But this principle is just as applicable to other problems that we face. If you are in financial trouble, you must begin by recovering from debt and then regain a level of financial comfort. If you are excessively self-critical, you must first learn to *separate from* (and disagree with) the negative messages, and then reconnect yourself *to* a positive self-image. (Separating from internal negative messages is covered more thoroughly in *The Self-Forgiveness Handbook*.)

Responding

What are some of the toxic elements of your life that you have already *recovered from?*

What do you know, or suspect, is toxic in your life now? Is it difficult for you to let go of it? Or does it feel more like it has a hold on you?

As you leave something negative behind, what are the positives you are moving *to?*

Dissatisfaction Can Be Your Fuel

Think of it this way: None of us would seek change or growth in our lives if we did not experience dissatisfaction. Dissatisfaction, in its many forms, ranging from excruciating pain to mild discomfort, is nothing more than the feeling that something is not as we would like it to be. We all use it all the time. When I shift positions in my chair, I am responding to dissatisfaction. When I drink a glass of water because I'm thirsty, I'm responding naturally to dissatisfaction.

On a larger scale, when we decide to change jobs or when we end a relationship, we are listening to and responding to our awareness of dissatisfaction. We're beginning a change by separating ourselves from what we consider to be the source of our discontent. We are negatively motivated—fueled by our dissatisfaction to move away from what is uncomfortable, toxic, or painful.

Why then was I concerned about my client Mitchell, who defined himself by those toxic behaviors he no longer engaged in? I was concerned because Mitchell had been involved in his recovery process for over fifteen years. More than fifteen years, and he was still "recovering from." He had not even begun to look for— *recover*—who he was beneath those negative behaviors. Mitchell knew who and what he was *not*, but he didn't have a clue as to who or what he was *instead*.

Motivation and Family Learning

Much of our personality is formed by unconscious decisions we make growing up. Experiences we have in our childhood influence us throughout our lives. This includes personal motivation; that is, what drives or doesn't drive us to our actions.

Motivation can work two ways. There is *positive motivation*, motivation born not of a need to *avoid* what has been previously, but of the need to *seek* what can be instead. And there is negative motivation, as I have just discussed. A woman in one of my seminars described the difference like this: "Negative motivation is being pushed from *behind* [the past], and positive motivation is being pulled from the *front* [the future]."

I wondered if Mitchell, having been pushed by—and defined by—his past for fifteen years, had ever felt the pull of his future. I began asking him questions about the future—specifically, what personal growth he envisioned for himself in that future. What I learned was that Mitchell was afraid to look ahead. He was almost superstitious about it, as if looking to his future would somehow jinx it. He participated in more than one twelve-step program and lived faithfully by the one day at a time principle. But his discomfort with looking toward the future was more than just a healthy focus in the present. Through a more in-depth exploration of Mitchell's fears, he and I eventually discovered the story that was underlying his insistence on defining himself by his past as well as his resistance to looking to his future.

Mitchell's mother had been very depressed for most of his child-hood. He remembered her primarily as lying on the sofa in their living room watching soap operas or sleeping. His father, on the other hand, was energetic and kept everything running smoothly for the family. Although he suspected that his father was angry about his mother's consistent inactivity, Mitchell never heard his father express such feelings. Mitchell described his father as being very adept at "working around" his mother.

Essentially, Mitchell experienced his mother as "the silent center of attention," around which everything in the family revolved. Looking back, he was able to determine that, probably much like his father, Mitchell was quite confused about his feelings for his mother. On the one hand, he felt a heavy sense of guilt, as if he was "supposed to know what to do" to make her feel better. On the other hand, he felt his mother's absence from his life. This left Mitchell feeling hurt, angry, and extremely negative about himself—as if there were something fundamentally wrong with him that kept her away. She was hospitalized (for depression presumably) on several occasions for anywhere from a few days to a week at a time. Mitchell realized as we talked that he had privately become ashamed of himself because when his mother was in the hospital, he had had such a sense of relief that she was out of the house. During the hospitalizations, not only was the house without the heaviness of his mother's depression, but his father seemed in a much better mood.

In one session Mitchell described his father as being like "one of those jugglers in the circus who keep all those plates spinning on the sticks." Between managing his own business, taking care of Mitchell and his younger brother, keeping house, and responding to his wife's needs, there was little or no extra time for his sons.

When Mitchell was in his second year of college, his mother began emerging from her depression for longer and longer periods of time. She even began to work part-time selling residential real estate. Sadly, his father was killed that year in a single-car accident. Mitchell suspected that his father had committed suicide but had never spoken with anyone about the possibility. I remember how Mitchell flip-flopped from crying to laughing during the session in which he spoke of how ironic it was to him that after all those years of his mother's depression, his father (possibly) committed suicide. While in this session, Mitchell described feeling "extremely emotionally confused."

By this time in his therapy, Mitchell understood that he only defined himself by the negative or toxic behaviors that he no longer engaged in and that he completely avoided anything resembling a purely positive statement about himself. The two of us were beginning to make sense out of it. Mitchell's identity was formed significantly by decisions that he made through the course of his childhood. For instance, he became aware of having made a strong, almost defiant, decision at a young age that no matter what, he was not going to be like his mother. That decision, once made, was immediately relegated to his unconscious mind because he would not be able to bear the guilt of such a strong negative feeling about his mother. Mitchell made the following life-changing decision at the time of his father's death: Seeing his father as such a good, hardworking man who devoted his life to taking care of others, only to die at the age of forty-seven, filled him with guilt. Mitchell decided that he didn't deserve the happiness and fulfillment that had evaded his father.

With this information, Mitchell's almost phobic avoidance of positive motivation made perfect sense. He was remaining faithful to the decision he had made when he was a young child, although he had not consciously remembered the decision. And his self-image as a man who doesn't engage in certain toxic behaviors made sense too; it was his way of honoring his childhood decision to *not* be like his mother.

Once Mitchell and I had covered this ground, rediscovering his formative decisions and talking about thoughts and feelings that he hadn't been able to express, he began to shift from his negatively motivated style toward new experiences with positive motivation. He recognized that although he had some characteristics similar to his mother, he was not at all like the mother of his childhood. Mitchell specifically—and completely consciously—*redecided* that he *did* deserve happiness and fulfillment even though his father had lived and died without those rewards. I remember Mitchell telling me in one of his last therapy sessions that he had decided to seek the pleasure that comes from living the good life both he and his father deserved.

The Hand-Off from Negative to Positive Motivation

Motivation is a lifelong challenge. It is too easy to get caught up in the requirements of our daily lives and forget about the importance of remaining motivated. I'm not talking about the motivation that gets us to the office each day because we need the paycheck. The motivation of a self-responsible person is a motivation to be fully alive, to be aware of your decisions and not to live a life by default. To have this motivation, we must be ready, willing, and able to turn our negative motivation into positive motivation. That is, once we have cleared ourselves of what has been damaging or toxic to us, we must turn our attention to what we want *instead*. Remember, with negative motivation, we decide who and what we are *not;* with positive motivation, we determine who and what we *are* and *will be.*

Responding

Are there decisions you have made along the way about what you will and will not do? Who you will and will not be? Is it time to reconsider any of those decisions now? Is it time to reinforce any of those decisions now?

What is one decision that you could make today that would help you to be positively motivated?

Extreme Motivation

Sometimes it's easier to become motivated in drastic circumstances. After life-threatening close calls, for instance, we will likely inventory our lives, reevaluating priorities, making new, life-affirming decisions. Fortunately, we don't have to wait for the near-death experiences or other close calls to inspire us toward such awakenings. When we are really paying attention, we can let others' and our own extreme experiences inspire us.

A few years ago I began working part-time at a local hospital in the organ transplant department. Having considerable experience working with addictive and compulsive behaviors and being a recovering alcoholic myself, I was brought on as an addiction consultant to the medical transplant team. Physicians, nurses, and social workers all worked on this team. These specialized professionals aren't only involved in preparing patients for and performing the transplant surgery, they also have the awesome responsibility of deciding who goes on—and when they go on—the transplant waiting list. My job is to help the team evaluate transplant candidates for possible addictive problems that can be problematic both before and after the transplant. When patients with addictive problems have been identified, my job is to help those patients develop and begin a sound recovery program.

I have been doing assessments for alcohol and drug addictions, and for eating disorders, for many years. When the need for some kind of treatment becomes apparent, the next question is this: *Why would this patient want to do something about this problem?* In other words, *where will the motivation to recover come from?*

To someone who has never experienced an addictive condition, this may seem like a silly question with obvious answers. *If something is wrong, then I want to fix it. If I am ill, then I will want to get well.* But because addiction is characterized by the presence of a psychological denial of either the existence of the problem or the severity of it, lighting the fire of motivation isn't always easy.

For many of the clients I've assessed over the years, their marriages, their jobs, their relationships with their children have been on the line. And for many of them, the threat of these serious consequences is enough to light the motivation fire. But for others, a turbulent marriage, a precarious job situation, or even an arrest for driving under the influence may not be enough to spark the flame.

The first thing that I noticed when I began the work at the hospital was that when a transplant candidate is diagnosed as having an addictive disorder, there is nothing subtle about the motivation to begin recovery. It is, in every case, their very lives at stake. *You need a new heart, and here is what you will need to do in order to be placed on the waiting list. . . .*

Now, that's motivation!

Motivation and Accountability: Disciplining Yourself

Our daily lives are not usually motivated by such dire circumstances, which is why we need some accountability. Two ways you can go about disciplining yourself to stay motivated are *external accountability* and *internal accountability*. Both of these methods are also linked directly to your sense of self-respect. When you hold yourself accountable for living up to your own expectations, which are congruent with your personal value system, you *earn your own respect*. If you want to start making proactive, responsible decisions in your life to act in ways that give you a stronger self-image, you will need to stay motivated.

The immediate consequences of our actions are often either not there or are not severe enough to scare us into stoking the motivational fire. Consider the following scenarios.

This morning I had planned to begin writing by 7:00 AM. As usual, I was running behind schedule, and I thought this would be a good day to try to catch up. I didn't wake up, however, until 7:30 (the first time), and since my cat was sleeping on my stomach, I went back to sleep. Of course, I didn't want to disturb the kitty. I was finally up and out of bed by 8:45. While in the kitchen making breakfast, I noticed that some dishes needed to be washed and that the floor could use some sweeping. When the kitchen was clean, I took my breakfast into the living room so I could mindlessly watch television while I ate. By 9:30 I had finished breakfast but was right in the middle of a "Bonanza" rerun. About 9:45 I heard my wife's car pull up in the driveway. Without the slightest concern for Little Joe's amnesia, I turned the television off, came upstairs, and turned on my computer.

Let's take a look at my morning in terms of motivation. All along, I was moving toward writing; I knew that I would eventually get here, in front of the computer. But when I woke up at 7:30, already thirty minutes past my planned starting time, all of my expectations flew out the window. This is a familiar feature of many of our minds: *all or none thinking*. All or none thinking is a wonderful tool for procrastinators; all we have to do is miss the mark by just a little, and we are off the hook. Once I was out of bed, I was still planning to write, and believe it or not, I was moving in that direction. You might say my motivational fire was on simmer.

The burst of motivational flame came with the sound of my wife's truck in the driveway because right below the surface of my procrastination is the knowledge (or awareness) of what I really need to be doing in order to respect myself. My wife was my reminder, or wake-up call. Not because she will berate me, or throw things at me, if I am not hard at work when she comes in. The truth is my wife would pay very little attention to whether I was upstairs at the computer or on the couch watching "Bonanza." What so quickly inspired me to abandon "Bonanza," and go to work was a little thing called *accountability*. Last night, I had told my wife about my early morning catch-up plan, and because she knew, and I knew that she knew, the sound of her truck threatened the secrecy of my lazy morning. Whether or not she cared one way or another, someone else would know that I had fallen short of my goal, and I would have to face *myself*—I had let myself down.

Of course, by acting as I did, I solved nothing. When my wife came in the house and I had been upstairs tapping away on the computer keyboard for a total of fifteen seconds, I was only presenting the illusion that I had followed through with my goal. (And keep in mind that I was presenting this illusion to someone who, very busy herself today, was probably not paying the slightest attention to my performance.) What is really demonstrated in this morning's scenario is my own discomfort when I lack discipline. Interestingly, but not surprising, when I was the only one who knew, that discomfort was not enough to get me moving. However, the moment that someone else (whose opinion of me I value) might know the truth of my morning, my motivation returned in full force. My wife, therefore, although an external component, served as a reminder of my own desire to uphold my self-respect.

There are a couple of solid pieces of information that we can extract from this simple story. First, including other people in your goal setting by increasing the sense of accountability (to them as direct witnesses to our behavior) is an excellent way to stoke the motivational fires. And second, it is important to be able to strengthen a sense of *internal accountability* (between self and self) so that you do not become dependent on the presence of others to keep you motivated.

External Accountability

When I work with people in individual psychotherapy who want to change certain attitudes or behaviors, accountability is one of the first things we talk about. Usually, by the time the person is sitting in the therapy room with me he has made many attempts at changing the designated problem on his own. As a drinking alcoholic, for instance, I cannot count the times that, as a drinking alcoholic, I made sincere decisions to cut back or stop drinking *on my own*, meaning *without telling anyone else.* When you don't tell anyone else, you don't have to admit *out loud* that you've not followed through. It is also easier to deny this to yourself when you have no one else to answer to.

And so I ask my clients about those times when they tried to change on their own. And I ask about their reluctance to tell other people about the plans to change. Inevitably, it boils down to their attempts to avoid embarrassment and shame. They don't want witnesses to their failures. This is completely understandable, and it is absolutely essential that we learn to override our fears and step to the plate of accountability to others. This is an important step in learning to take responsibility for ourselves.

Accountability to others has to do with being responsible to those other people as well, as discussed in chapter one. When you need to be accountable to another person because of the nature of your relationship with that person (such as a family member or friend) or the nature of an agreement with that person (such as a business arrangement or a specific agreement with someone), that sense of accountability will, of course, be motivating for most of you.

But it is also charged with other relationship meanings, such as *trust-worthiness* and *integrity*, which are also usually linked to your sense of self-respect. If you are struggling with this kind of accountability, I suggest that you review the material in chapter one, focusing on what it means to be responsible *to* another person.

Another kind of accountability involving others is what I call *The Positive Use of Tattling*. To use this kind of accountability to stoke the motivational fires, when you decide to make a change, you simply *tell on yourself*. Tell at least one other person who you know cares about you, someone who doesn't feel the need to control your efforts to change and who won't support you in making excuses if you drop the ball.

This is the kind of accountability I always want to make good use of as a psychotherapist. When a client doesn't follow through successfully with a plan made in an earlier session, it won't do her any good to lie to me about it or to avoid the subject. In fact, she may ultimately make more progress by failing to do the planned task and talking about it in the next session. Most of us can use the experience of not being harshly judged for falling short of our goals. Eventually we can even learn to stop condemning ourselves for our human imperfection, learn from the mistake, and give it another shot.

Responding

How have you used external accountability as motivation?

Are you currently struggling with a problem that might be helpful if you "told on yourself" to someone you trust?

Internal Accountability

I don't think that we should ever shed the need for external accountability. Communicating with others about what you are doing in your life is a simple yet powerful way to remain connected to others, and knowing how and when to "tell on yourself" is a useful tool for your toolbox.

A good example of this comes from a choice I made about three months ago. I decided to stop smoking cigars. I had come to realize that what I had once characterized as an occasional pleasure had become a full-blown addiction. (I am an extremely talented and versatile addict.) For about a week and a half after I stopped smoking, I didn't mention what I was doing to anyone. I knew at the time that I was doing the same thing I had done with alcohol all those years ago: By attempting to stop but not telling anyone around me, I was protecting my ability to return to my friends, the cigars. And I knew that if I did not tell someone, it would only be a matter of time until I returned to my newest addiction.

What it took for me to create some external accountability was some of my own *internal accountability*. The original conversation inside my head went something like this:

Decision Maker: I know this isn't good for me. No, it's worse than that. Smoking cigars, especially as much as I am smoking, is bad for me ... dangerous for me. I'm going to stop smoking cigars.

Addiction Protector: No you're not. You don't smoke *that* much. If you are concerned about it, just cut back some.

Decision Maker: Well, yeah, I could just stop smoking as many as ... no, wait a minute. You and I have had this conversation before. No way. I'm quitting.

Addiction Protector: Whatever. But you have half a box of good cigars left. You sure can't quit until they are gone; that would be a waste.

Decision Maker: You're not going to get me with that one. I remember how many times you told me that I could quit drinking when the bottle was empty. None of those bottles were ever empty! I can throw the cigars away, or give them to somebody, or something. I am quitting, starting today, starting right now.

Addiction Protector: Okay, fine. We'll see how it goes. You're the boss.

Decision Maker: I know you don't believe it, but I *am* the boss. I am going to stop smoking cigars, and I am going to tell Gary [my business partner] and Dede [my wife].

Addiction Protector: Okay, you can do that if that's what you want. But what if you decide just to smoke a couple more before you throw them out? Or what if, with the weather starting to warm up, you want to see if it's possible to have an occasional cigar while you sit out on the porch in the evenings?

Decision Maker: [thinking] Mmmmm.

Addiction Protector: You can see I'm right, can't you?

Decision Maker: No, I'm not fooled. I know exactly what you
                      are doing. And I know that I shouldn't listen
                      to you. But you're right about me wanting to
                      keep those other options open.

Addiction Protector: Yes, you do.

Decision Maker: Okay, I won't mention it to anyone just yet . . .
                      but I am quitting.

Addiction Protector: I know you are. I understand.

Can you see how I am not getting to utilize the external
accountability because of my lack of internal accountability? Knowing
exactly what I must do if I am serious about my goal, I am talked
down by The Addiction Protector. Notice how clever he is, how he
remains calmly in control (of *himself* and *me*) and how he easily settles
for just keeping his foot in the door. He knows that if I don't tell anyone about my intention to quit smoking, it will only be a matter of
time before he will have me smoking again.

Here is another internal conversation that occurred about a
week later, sitting in the kitchen with Dede:

Decision Maker: Quick, tell her. The Addiction Protector is look-
                      ing the other way!

Thom to *Dede:*   *I haven't had a cigar in over a week.*

Addiction Protector: You idiot!

Dede: *That's great. Why haven't you?*

Decision Maker: Hurry! Finish it. Tell her you're quitting.

Thom: *Well, of course I can't predict the future, and I've
                      learned to never say never, but I intend to quit. I
                      have realized that your and everyone else's concerns
                      about my health are real, and I don't want to die of
                      cancer, or have my jaw rot off, and look back and
                      think, "If only I would have quit. . . ."*

Dede: *I'm glad. I know you're probably going to miss
                      your cigars.*

Thom: *Oh well, but I can do it. It helps just for me to let
                      you know.*

Addiction Protector: You're damned right it helps. You blew it. You are going to be sorry. I'm out of here, but *I'll be back.*

It's not pretty, but there you have it: an example of some internal accountability. What I have learned over the years is that sometimes getting the job done means being an opportunist, always ready to scoop up what must be done and run with it. Sometimes, being accountable to ourselves will feel like doing and saying things in spite of ourselves. That's why I call it *The Positive Use of Tattling.*

Responding

Write your own inner dialogue about a personal struggle for internal accountability. Use your imagination. Have fun with it.

7

Power

Taking Your Life into Your Own Hands

Janice was not unusual in her hesitation to connect her current problems to her early relationship with her parents. She was, however, more adamant than most. "I don't see how our relationship could possibly have to do with anything I am experiencing now," she told me flatly within the first twenty minutes of her initial consultation. She continued, "I am here to solve problems of my own. These are not my parents' problems; I am sure not blaming them for anything that is going on with me in my adult life."

"I am not suggesting that we blame your parents for . . ." I began to respond.

"People who come to therapy to lay the blame on their parents are pitiful in my opinion," Janice continued, unaware that I had begun to speak. She was on a roll.

One of the lessons I have learned as a psychotherapist is to recognize when a client is *not* asking for my opinion. In professional training workshops, I teach other therapists that they can save themselves a lot of headaches by recognizing when the door in front of them is closed. For the time being, I would just listen and hear Janice out.

Nonetheless, in many ways I agree with Janice. Good psycho-therapy is not about blaming others for your problems—parents or anyone else. Good psychotherapy is about taking responsibility for yourself; it's about taking charge of your own life. It's about return-ing the power of your life to the proper owner—*you*. Unfortunately for Janice, to accomplish that she was going to have to return to her past. Although you don't want to be the helpless victim of your past, you do want to understand how it has affected your current attitudes and behaviors. With this awareness, you then have the power to adjust and change. I remember, several weeks into her therapy, tell-ing her something I had heard a friend of mine say: *Blame is nice place to visit, you just don't want to live there.* Janice laughed.

Power and Your Past

When you begin to look into your origins, be sure to know something of what you are looking for. Certainly, you want to remain flexible and open to the unexpected, but you should at least understand the purpose of exploring your past. The point of exploring the past is not to find someone to blame, but to better understand a problem so that it can be effectively solved.

Like Janice, many of us need to think about the experiences of our childhoods so that we can learn more about how we came to be the way we are. Specifically, I encouraged Janice to discover what she could about how her parents *defined and used power*. This seemed the appropriate direction to give her for a couple of reasons. First, Jani-ce's objections were so strong that it made me wonder what she might be afraid of. It was like she had frantically thrown her back against a door, saying, "There's nothing in here! No need to look here!" before I had a chance to really even ask. And second, when she did begin to trust me enough for us to talk a little about her parents, she seemed to swing from one extreme to another—from seeming extremely impatient and angry with them to becoming enormously protective of them. Soon I stopped thinking that she was trying to protect her parents from me or from therapy. Janice was trying to protect her parents from herself. She was afraid of the powerful mix of emotions that began to stir when we discussed her family.

Identifying Problem Sources

Any of the core emotions that become toxic to us when they cannot find full and natural expression—fear, anger, shame, guilt—

can be traced back to exposure to inappropriate, abusive, or ineffective use of power. Consider the following examples:

David *hears increasing complaints from family, friends, and co-workers that he is difficult to get along with, that he has become extremely irritable and snappy with people. When asked, David says that I "never really get angry." In therapy we discover that he is inwardly involved in an almost constant struggle against mounting rage, and we trace this dysfunctional relationship with anger back to a loud and aggressive father who seemed "mad at the world." David's father consistently shut down the first signs of anger (even frustration) in his children by instantly becoming angrier than they were. As a child it didn't take David long to learn that feeling anger "was useless" and that expressing it would "only make matters worse."*

Scott *is prone to "shame attacks," intense and excruciating shameful feelings that come on rapidly, sometimes with only the slightest provocation. He doesn't associate his problem with his family of origin, which he describes as "not perfect, but pretty normal, and definitely stable." When asked to think back to the very first "shame attack" that he can remember, Scott describes a humiliating experience when he was in the seventh grade (as if being in the seventh grade isn't painful enough), in which an English teacher embarrassed him in front of the class for not having adequately prepared for an oral report. Scott's teacher told him that she was "making an example" of him. Scott would discover other such embarrassing incidents that would reinforce this "programming," but it was the seventh-grade English teacher who represented the origin of his shame attacks.*

Shirley *is a perfectionist. According to her (impossible) standards, she can never do anything well enough. She describes a pervasive feeling of guilt as her "constant companion" through life. Recently, in family therapy, Shirley has been confronted with a pattern of manipulation to get what she wants. The constant guilt, perfectionism, and manipulation are traced back to the following family-of-origin dynamics. Shirley was the youngest of three sisters (it was the three sisters who had come together for a series of therapy sessions, shortly after their mother's death). Shirley was, in the opinion of her sisters, their parents' favorite child. The two sisters said, almost in unison, "Shirl was their little girl!" Being placed on a pedestal by her parents and feeling the resentment from her sisters, she became strongly identified with feelings of guilt—because she knew that she would never be able to live up to her parents' "perfect" image of her (she felt like a fraud) and*

*because she always thought that she was taking something away
from her sisters, something that she didn't deserve. Shirley's
mother was a master of manipulation, and since Shirley could not
acknowledge her own needs (that would make her less than perfect), she modeled herself after her mother, learning to manipulate
to get her needs met. Of course, when her needs were met, she
would feel guilty, undeserving, and fraudulent.*

I encourage my clients and workshop audiences to think of their
families not in terms of function or dysfunction, but instead in the
simple terms of learning from the problems. Consider the family you
grew up in to be your alma mater, the school where you originally
learned about the world and how to be in it.

For instance, in the previous example, David was in a much better position to make the changes he needed to make once he understood that his own anger had been shut down by his father's anger.
He realized that as long as he did not step up and take responsibility
for identifying and expressing his anger, it would only continue to
"slip out sideways," alienating the people around him.

Scott's shame attacks didn't cease, but they did decrease in fre-
quency and intensity. It proved helpful to him to see how his shame
attacks made sense, that he came by the problem honestly. Scott told
me that he needed that reassurance so that he could stop thinking of
himself as hysterical and crazy. Scott also discovered that he had
needed his parents to stand up for him when he was humiliated at
school but they had either thought it best to let him handle it on his
own or had not realized how devastating the effect of that experience
had been for their son. With this awareness, Scott realized that part of
his healing would be about his learning to stand up for himself and
not automatically assume (with the first sense of shame) that he had
done anything wrong at all.

Shirley is in the midst of her therapy. Understanding how her
family dynamics relate to her unrealistic demands upon herself has
helped her come up with the following clear and important challenges for herself:

1. Setting realistic goals (within the realm of possibility) and
   recognizing when a goal has been achieved.

2. Writing a letter of resignation from the family position "pedestal child." (She is writing this in her private journal, but she
   does plan to share it with her sisters.)

3. Identifying personal needs, acknowledging that having needs
   only means that she is alive and human, and practicing asking directly for those needs to be met.

And remember Janice, who insisted on not falling into the trap of blaming her parents for her behavior as an adult? Well, I knocked on the door occasionally, but for the most part, I waited patiently for an opportunity to catch a glimpse of what she had learned at her alma mater.

Responding

Who was powerful in your home when you were growing up? How was power demonstrated or used?

What are two or three things you learned about your power while you were growing up?

Describe each of your parents' style of demonstrating power.

Errant Power

We all have power—it's natural. But personal power is a lot like money: Having it is one thing, managing it is quite another.

The scenarios above (David, Scott, and Shirley) are good examples of how misused power begets misused power. From one generation to the next, distorted perceptions of personal power have been passed down. One of the positive results of this psychotherapy age in which we live may be that we have the opportunity to interrupt these long-standing, and quite harmful, traditions.

We live in a world that interprets power in many different ways. As a result, we each grow up with our own variation of an erroneous (at least) or destructive (at worst) understanding of this thing called power. To become fully responsible, most of us have to undergo major revisions of that understanding. The first step in making those revisions is to become aware of the various misuses and abuses of power that we are likely to have encountered or practiced. The following are two categories of managing power that can prove counterproductive, harmful, or even destructive. Consider each of these in terms of yourself and in terms of other people who have been influential in your life. Ask yourself this realistic, beneficial question: *How do these categories of misused power apply to me and people I know?*

Power to Dominate. This is the blatant use of personal power *against* or *over* other people. This can be accomplished with a multitude of strategy and style differences, including intimidation, undermining, and withholding. Here are some examples:

- *Withholding*—A mother who uses her silence and aloofness to punish others in the family to exert her control.

- *Intimidation*—An employer who regularly holds his employees' jobs over their heads as a way of maintaining control.

- *Undermining*—A parent whose first response to a child's accomplishment is, "Great, but you could have done even better."

Power to Manipulate. This is a more *covert* use of power to gain control of other people by indirect means. The use of power to manipulate will include fostering the dependence of others, feigning powerlessness or incompetence, and imposing guilt on others. Here are some examples:

- *Fostering dependence*—A father who continues to be responsible for his daughter's finances well into her young adulthood.

- *Feigning incompetence*—A woman who, in the name of being complimentary, avoids taking on responsibilities by telling others, "You are so much better at that than I am."

- *Imposing guilt*—A man who uses body language and facial expressions, such as sulking, to express perpetual disappointment.

Whatever the strategy or style, the person who uses power to dominate defines power in reference to the lack of other people's power. "It's not enough that I should win, you must lose" might be the applicable motto here. The person who expresses power through manipulation constantly comes from a "one down" position and often will not be consciously aware of his misuse of power.

The one common denominator in all of these errant uses of power is *mistaking these uses of power for control.* When we are in possession of our personal power, we are not in control. There is a very big difference. Remember, being in charge is the desired position, in which we *accept full responsibility for our decisions* and remain aware of all that we do not and cannot control.

Responding

List some examples of your expressing power through manipulation or attempts to dominate.

Consider how you have equated power with control.

How do you want to use your power in your life?

A New Kind of Power: Taking Responsibility

Genuine power comes from within us. Genuine power has nothing to do with controlling other people or getting what we need through manipulation. Genuine power is our birthright: No person gives it to us, and no person has the right to take it from us. Genuine power is the power to make our own choices, not hiding behind a shield of victimization (*I had no choice, I had to do it*). Genuine power is the power—and the courage—to step forward and claim full responsibility for ourselves, mistakes and all.

The Old Adult: The Image

I remember when my image of being an adult had more to do with how I dressed, what kind of job I had, and how I appeared to other people than it did with how I was thinking and feeling about myself. And I remember that in those days I never really felt like an adult. I felt like a child masquerading as an adult; I felt like a fraud. Every day was potentially the day when someone would finally discover me—the true me, the twelve-year-old impostor me. "Ahha!" someone would say, "I see who you are. You are no adult. You are nothing more than an incompetent little kid. How dare you try to fool me like this!" I would, of course, be humiliated, but I wouldn't blame my confronter. After all, it was the truth: I was a fake.

I would remain a fake for as long as I tried to become an adult from the outside in—trying to fulfill the image I had of what it meant to be an adult. To complicate matters more, for as long as my goal was to step into that image, I would vehemently resist reaching my own goal. There was very little about that adult image that I found attractive; I just thought it was necessary. So it went for years, the perpetual, isometric tug-a-war within, one part of me pulling with all its might toward "being an adult," and another part, with at least equal strength, pulling in the opposite direction, screaming "No way!"

The New Adult: From the Inside Out

Today, there are a couple of good tug-a-wars going on in this land I call my mind, but there is no tug-a-war about whether or not I will be an adult or what it means to be an adult. I am proud to say that neither side won. Today, being an adult has nothing to do with how I dress and very little to do with what other people think of me. But I am an adult.

The victim's condition at any time can be determined more by the external circumstances than by anything within himself. The victim's charge is to control the outside circumstances or to be defeated. A really good victim won't even try to control the circumstances, but will just wait to change on their own or for someone to come along who will change them.

I live with—and now teach others—a new definition for this small but ominous word, "adult." My new definition for "adult" is the person who recognizes that his well-being (or lack thereof) is determined more by his *responses* to the external circumstances than by the circumstances themselves.

Alcoholics Anonymous' *Serenity Prayer* is good advice to live by, whether we are particularly prone to prayer or not:

> *God grant me the serenity*
> *to accept the things I cannot change,*
> *the courage to change the things I can,*
> *and the wisdom to know the difference.*

A fully responsible adult can live according to this principle. That doesn't mean that as an adult, I am perfect in this application. Far from it. To live according to *The Serenity Prayer* means that I have placed it at the center of my thinking, that I believe in its effectiveness in helping me to resolve conflicts within myself, and that when I lose my place, become confused, or distracted, I will remember to return to the center of my thinking, where I keep this little gem. It will bail me out every time.

Another way I have come to think about being an adult is this: *I am the person who is 100 percent responsible for me. I am the healthy parent to the child within me.* One hundred percent responsible leaves no room for blaming anyone for anything. I explained to Janice that being a healthy parent to herself was just another metaphor for being responsible for herself. When I promised Janice that my intention was to make certain that she remain 100 percent responsible, no matter what we might discover in her past, she finally agreed to tell me a little about her family.

Responding

Describe a time when you felt like an "impostor."

Write your own definition of being an adult.

Describe yourself as an adult.

Family Power: Breaking the Ties That Bound Us

Whether Janice liked it or not, whether you or I like it or not, the environments we grow up in have a lot to do with the adults we become. And of all of the lessons we learn from our families—directly, indirectly, even covertly—there are none that will have as great an effect on us as those experiences that teach us about the use of personal power. How you perceive your relationship with power will determine, probably more than anything else, how you will interact with others in the course of your life. So whether we like it or not, looking into the lessons of power is a requirement when we plan to make any significant change in ourselves.

Janice discovered as we talked that she didn't know much about her father. He worked a lot, she said, but even when he was around the house, he was distant. Janice thought her father worried a lot. He worked for a large investment firm; thinking back on it now, she assumes that his mind was on his work most of the time. As a child, however, she had felt somehow responsible for her father's distant moods. She told me that she had not felt as much like she caused his distancing as she felt strongly that she should be able to help in some way to make him feel better.

"That's natural," I told Janice. "When something is distracting or disturbing a parent, children will often feel responsible if they are not given enough information to let them know otherwise. Children want to make their parents feel better for a couple of very good reasons: First, they love their parents, and second, they need the love of the parents to be demonstrated. It's simple; we all want to love and we all want to be loved."

Janice told me later that she believed I was reassuring her in order to trick her into giving me information about her parents and that as soon as she did, I would "pounce," telling her how they were to blame for all of her problems. Once she realized that I wasn't waiting to ambush her parents, she actually seemed to enjoy coming to therapy. She was very relieved.

Janice did experience occasionally what she called her "post-therapy paranoid episodes," during which she would feel big waves of guilt for talking to me about her family. "I feel so bad about myself," Janice said as she described one of these episodes.

"Do you feel disloyal, like you've broken some code of honor?" I asked.

Janice raised her head and looked at me. "Yes. That's exactly what it feels like."

"Well, there is good news and bad news," I began. "The bad news is that you probably have violated some major unspoken agreement you made with your family. The good news is that breaking away from the hold that agreement has had on you is necessary if you want to claim your life as your own."

"I don't know if I'm going to be able to do this part," Janice said, looking worried. "Whatever this is, it feels much stronger than me."

Janice had become aware of something many of us have to face along the path to personal responsibility. Her family was very proud and very private. She and her sisters were told on a number of occasions, and in a number of ways, that they were not to speak to anyone of anything less than perfect about the family. It was clear that to do so would be a betrayal of the family. This explained the dilemma Janice was in when she first came to therapy. She wanted to feel better, to take care of herself, but to do so, she was going to have to break one of her family's laws.

She was now aware of that dilemma. Janice saw herself at a crossroads; one road led to her well-being and the betrayal of her family, and the other road was the continuation of the road she had been on until now. Neither choice was good. Janice loved her family, so taking the road to her own well-being would not be easy for her; she would feel so badly about violating the family honor code that she would no doubt be miserable. "This isn't a crossroads," she told me. "This is a dead end!"

Her parents lived at least a thousand miles away from that therapy session, but they controlled it nevertheless. Or more accurately, the satellites of themselves that had become implanted in Janice's mind were in control. What she didn't know was that she stood right at the very edge of her freedom—the freedom to pursue her own happiness and the freedom to love her parents. This wasn't a cross-roads; it was a launching pad.

The Stronger Power: You

The lie that was keeping Janice from moving was this one: *There are two choices, and you can only choose one.*

I asked Janice, "What do you think about the idea of continuing to love and honor your parents and learning to love and honor your-self as well?"

"Easy for you to say," she responded quickly.

"I really do believe that you can have both. I don't believe that you have to choose between yourself and your family. In fact, I refuse to believe it. If you remain stuck here, it is because you are limiting your thinking, not because your choices are limiting you."

Honoring a contract is generally a very good thing. But when we look closely at the "contracts of silence" or "contracts of perfec-tion" that we often discover in our families, I think we are talking more about rules that have been imposed on us than on agreements in which we have participated. This is not to say our parents are vil-lains; most of them are not. These family codes of honor are, more often than not, some version of family beliefs that have been passed from one generation to another, without anyone taking the time to reevaluate them. And these family "don't talk" rules are seldom fueled with any malice. They are fueled by fear: the fear of their fraud being discovered and the fear of change. That fear of change is the fear of the unknown and the unfamiliar. It is so much easier to take the paths of least resistance—the roads heavily traveled.

The power that most of us grow up knowing about is *defensive power*. This kind of power is used to keep us from being revealed as impostors, to dominate or manipulate others so that we can last another day. Too often, when we look closely at what we know about and how we use our personal power, we will discover that we are using our power to survive life rather than live it.

Personal power becomes stronger when we stop using it to sur-vive by attempting to control something that we cannot possibly con-trol, or something that is none of our business, and begin to use it in proactive, self-caring ways. Personal power becomes stronger when it is fueled by desire, belief, and hope rather than fear, anger, and shame. And personal power transcends the crossroads where Janice stood, trying to choose between two pretty undesirable options.

In the case of breaking the family codes, personal power that is benevolent and constructive will not destroy anyone. Over the course of a little more than a year, Janice told me many things about her family, and much of what she told me was not very flattering, to say the least. But what she told me was the truth, and telling it played a significant role in freeing Janice to become the person she wanted to be. It was as if the law of family loyalty had sent her out into life with both arms tied behind her back. She just needed some help getting them untied.

Sometimes clients will ask one or both of their parents to join them for a few therapy sessions somewhere down the line. Janice thought about it, but she eventually decided that she didn't feel ready to be that vulnerable with either one of her parents. I'm sure it was a good decision.

Janice became quite an expert at identifying her needs and desires and then making choices to fulfill them. To a large extent, she accomplished this by examining what she learned from her parents—how their relationships with her, with each other, and even with themselves had contributed to Janice's self-perception, self-esteem, and personal expectations. I remember commenting to Janice one day, "Have you noticed that we've been talking about you and your family for several months now, and neither one of your parents has been damned to hell—by me, you, or anyone else?"

"I never doubted you for a moment." She smiled.

Responding

What rule from your family of origin do you need to break?

What is your greatest fear about breaking a family rule?

What is your greatest hope?

8

Purpose

Discovering What Gives You Direction

When I began my training as a psychotherapist, I envisioned my work as involving deep conversations with my clients about "the meaning of life." Together, we would respond to the existential angst inherent in the human condition by peeling layer after layer from the proverbial onion. We would come to understand the understandable, we would marvel at the mysteries that we could not comprehend, and we would stand face-to-face with the inevitable: *human mortality*.

Seventeen years later, I have spent plenty of time talking with clients about the existential matters I originally hoped for. But these substantial conversations about the meaning of life have not presented themselves in the form that I expected when I was in graduate school. Clients do not show up on my doorstep with philosophical discussions in mind; they come for help with problems. They aren't seeking deep conversation; they want solutions. And I have discovered that when I can respond directly to their needs and when I am willing and able to listen carefully to what they have to say, I will come to understand what is important to each of them. I have learned that there is a conversation that is far more important than the one about the meaning of life. It is the conversation that is about the meaning of each of our individual lives—the meaning of *his* life, and *her* life, and *your* life, and *my* life.

Every one of those conversations is unique, and underlying every one of those stories is a need (fulfilled or not) for a sense of purpose, a way of giving meaning to who we are and what we do.

For example, for a certain middle-aged woman, her purpose may be recognizing a lifelong destructive pattern of victimization and then choosing to leave an abusive relationship and pursue her dream of a postgraduate degree and a professional career. Or a young man, being confronted with the addictive nature of a series of relationships, makes a commitment to remain out of relationship and celibate for a period of six months while he explores the emotions that are driving his compulsive tendencies. Another man, recognizing that he was emotionally (and often physically) absent as his three children grew up, plans a visit to each of his now grown children to tell them what he has learned and listen to what they have to say to him.

It is important for you to identify a sense of purpose as part of becoming a fully responsible person. That purpose doesn't have to be a directive from God or a certain mission to be accomplished before your dying day. A healthy sense of purpose is flexible and changing. What I tell you about purpose in my life today and what I tell you in two years may be different—or exactly the same. It's about feeling in touch with whatever gives your life meaning.

A sense of purpose is the awareness of your own significance, as an individual and in relationship to the world around you. It isn't necessary that you *name* your purpose. Experiencing a sense of purpose is knowing that you have value and that you belong where you are. In other words, experiencing your purpose is living in congruence with your personal value system.

Questions to Ask Yourself about Your Purpose

What am I doing here? What is the meaning of my life? What do I believe in? and What is it that makes me uniquely me?

These are not questions that lend themselves to short answers— or even single answers, for that matter. Here is an exercise that I have suggested to clients. Pose the first question to yourself, written on a small piece of paper (*What am I doing here?*). Carry the written question with you for a week. Keep it in your pocket or purse. You may want to get it out and look at it now and again, but more important, remember that you have the question with you at all times. Ask the question of yourself whenever you think of it. Don't work hard to find answers; instead, pay attention to any and all of the answers that you become aware of. Think of this not as a question with one correct answer, but as a question that acts as a magnet, attracting many appropriate answers. Collect those answers during the one week you carry the question with you.

You may discover that the question will have a different meaning, or at least different inferences, depending on what you're thinking about when you ask the question. For instance, when you remember the question while you're at work, you may discover answers related specifically to why you are in your particular job or why you have chosen your career. When you ask the question while you're considering a relationship with another person, you may find that your answers are about why you are in this particular relationship. Keep a pocket-size notebook with you so that you can write down some of your more interesting responses to the question.

At the end of one week, discard the first question and do the same with the second question (*What is the meaning of my life?*) Don't worry if some of your responses to one question overlap or repeat with another question. In fact, a response that shows up more than once or twice is probably worth noticing.

At the end of the second week, discard the second and pick up the third question (*What do I believe in?*) Finally, for the fourth week, carry the last question with you (*What makes me uniquely me?*)

Have fun with the exercise. Don't think of it as something you can do right or wrong, but just something you're considering. If you want to tell some people what you are up to, do so. Maybe you have a friend who will join you in the experiment. Think about extending the experiment a week or two with questions of your own. Or if it feels right, revise the questions that I have suggested.

Responding

Write and title a story or an essay reflecting on what you have learned from collecting responses to the questions above.

Defining Purpose

Because "purpose" is such an elusive concept, don't worry about it if these definitions aren't coming together right away. Each time I have been tempted to skip this discussion, someone says something to remind me that the sense of purpose—whether or not it is definable—is at the very core of our being.

For instance, as I was facilitating a workshop once, I asked the group of participants what part "a sense of purpose" played in their lives. "It's everything," one man said instantly. Another participant, a young woman, said, "It is purpose that I have been seeking my whole life. That's why I'm here in this workshop today. I need to know that I have a purpose."

I thought maybe these people could help me find *the* definition for "purpose"; they didn't, but they did help me to *characterize* it with a bit more depth. Here are some of the thoughts and associations that these workshop participants had about purpose:

Feeling a sense of purpose can give you direction in life.

Without purpose, nothing else can matter.

Purpose comes from deep inside each of us; it is our life force.

Purpose is what guides us—like something God implanted in each of us.

Understanding your purpose comes from knowing yourself on a deep fundamental level. It is about allowing that essence to guide you and your reactions.

Once again, I could see that this discussion could not be ignored. There is something about this thing called purpose that seems integral to our very existence. Therefore, you need to somehow identify your purpose in order to take responsibility for living according to it, thus earning your own respect.

A Mission Statement

To have purpose is to have concern for ourselves and the world around us. In fact, many people will describe one or two central concerns that are constants in their lives, such as a love for animals, a belief in a spiritual path, the desire to teach, or the connection with family and close friends. Purpose as a central concern doesn't have to be about saving the world from some terrible injustice; you just need to be responsible for yourself and for your relationships. Purpose, expressed in the form a central concern, becomes an organizing principle of your life—much like a business's mission statement.

With a clear mission statement, an organization always has an effective means of evaluating its foundation. For instance, if the mission statement of a particular establishment includes a commitment to contributing to the community in which it prospers, it becomes a relatively simple matter to see if contributions (in the forms of personal service and financial assistance) are being made.

You can benefit similarly from mission statements. They give you direction and a tangible way of evaluating your congruence with that direction.

The following are examples of an organizational mission statement, and then two personal mission statements, written by participants at a recent workshop. Notice that the mission statement is one of general direction more than it is of specific objectives. Mission statements help us to set a course and to evaluate our progress. A mission statement is analogous to telling myself that I plan on traveling north and northwest. With that information, it will be easy to see how I am doing. If I discover later that I am traveling south, then I can ask myself, "Am I off course, or have I changed my mind about what course I plan to take?"

Mission Statement from Alive Hospice, Inc., Nashville, Tennessee

Alive Hospice, Inc., will provide physical, psychological, and spiritual comfort and support to dying patients and their families, continuing during the time of bereavement, and will provide educational services and training related to life-threatening illness and grief to individuals and groups.

Personal Mission Statement #1

I have a primary focus on treating others well and acting in ways that encourage others to treat me with the same consideration. While taking full responsibility for my decision making, I will pursue personal success in my career, relationship, and personal health (mentally, physically, and spiritually).

Personal Mission Statement #2

I am committed to living a life that is productive for myself and others. I will be clear about my personal value system and live according to those values. In addition to productivity, my levels of relaxation and joy will play a significant part in evaluating my success.

Responding

Write your mission statement.

It can be clarifying to write a mission statement that you believe would have applied to your life at a time when you were being less responsible. For instance, for the years prior to 1986, I could write: I *am committed to being a productive professional and a responsible partner in my relationships, yet still refusing to treat my alcoholic dependency.*

Quality of Life— What It Means to You

Think back for a moment to chapter 5 and congruence, in which we discussed the important difference between living by decision and living by default. Remember realizing how easy it is to slip into living by default when you're not paying attention? Considering points like those in the this Responding Exercise is one effective way of keeping your Decision Maker awake at the wheel. These questions, and infinite others that we can create, put us directly in touch with the quality of our lives.

When you're bombarded with the unattainable standards that the media and the world of entertainment subject you to, you may be thinking of quality of life in terms of money, glamour, big houses, power, and more money. But even if we aspire to some—or all—of those things, when the television is turned off, most of us are clearly aware that quality of life is not about those material possessions or status symbols of Hollywood or Washington, D.C.

Life without Meaning: Letting Depression Take Over

Unfortunately, there are people who never get beyond their circumstances and remain trapped. Take note of the following story as a reminder—*stay aware,* and make the effort to change your actions. Get familiar with what gives you purpose. Let that, not your problems be your guidance. A woman named Beth attended one of my workshops many years ago. The workshop was about recovering from depression. I remember speaking directly to Beth, who was sitting in the front row: "What do you believe in? Tell me just one thing you believe in." I had done this little demonstration many times before, and I was assuming that I would once again, by way of my demonstration, teach the audience a "little trick" for intervening on a depressive episode. But first, I needed the assistance of someone in the audience. So I asked Beth my standard question, "What do you believe in?"

Beth was slumped in her chair, and there was a kind of flat look in her eyes—depression. But I had noticed that she had been paying very close attention to what I had to say that evening. She seemed like the perfect person to ask, "What do you believe in?"

She thought for a moment—I think just to be polite to me, pretending that she had to think of an answer—and then she said, "Nothing."

"Nothing?" I said. "That's pretty bleak." I pushed on. "Now this doesn't have to be anything big, like God or the United States of America. Just any little thing that you have a positive belief in . . . like the sun coming up in the morning."

"The sun coming up in the morning?" Beth asked, the depression in her eyes looking right at me.

"Yeah, like the sun coming up in the morning. Do you believe in that?" This will work, I thought.

"But you said something 'positive' that I believe in," Beth said.

The little demonstration I had become so proud of was going right down the drain. "Yes, something, any little thing that you have a positive belief in."

"Then I'll have to stick with nothing." Beth smiled as she answered. She was telling the truth, but she did have a sense of humor and could see the bitter irony of her answer.

In those days I was still pretty green in the public speaking department, and I very much appreciated that Beth was gracious enough to put her sense of humor into play and let me off the hook. Beth had helped me to abandon my little demonstration and move on and share with the audience how important it is to have something to believe in, to have meaning in our lives.

The rest of the evening went pretty well, and after I had finished, Beth was even among those who came up to shake my hand and thank me. At the time, I couldn't imagine what she appreciated in what I had said. I drove home thinking about Beth. After that, I didn't think of her anymore until she called my office about two years later.

Beth had called to ask if I would see her sixteen-year-old son in therapy. He had been drinking quite a lot, and Beth wasn't sure what other drugs he might be into, so she wanted my help in evaluating the situation. We made the appointment for the following day.

That appointment began a long association between Beth and me. I evaluated her son for problems with alcohol and drugs and referred him to a local residential treatment program. Over the next few years, I worked with Beth's son in individual therapy off and on, I saw their entire family for several sessions, and eventually Beth began coming for weekly individual sessions. She had already begun seeing an excellent psychiatrist for antidepressant medication, which helped her to stay out of "the valley of death," as she called it. Beth and I both worked hard during her son's therapy sessions, but the results of our work were few and far between. If I ever began to feel overconfident as a therapist, I would just think of my work with Beth and her family, and my humility would come rushing back to me.

I always enjoyed talking with Beth, and I think we formed a good, trusting relationship during our therapy hours together. We certainly enjoyed each other's sense of humor—once, for my birthday, she dropped a box of Betty Crocker cake mix off at my office, with a note saying that she was sorry that the cake was *a little under- done*. But other than being someone who cares about her (that usually counts for something), I don't think I have ever helped her.

Beth has come and gone from therapy a couple of times now, so I suppose she may be back for another round yet. I will sometimes write her a note on fliers about my workshops that go out from my office, and she will leave a phone message responding to the note, but other than that, I haven't heard from her in over two years now.

Here is what I *know* about Beth: From the day she was born, she has led a life devoid of love and kindness. Her parents were both extremely depressed (and untreated) and offered their children noth- ing more than the basics of food, clothing, and shelter. Beth fre- quently pointed to the fact that those basic needs were met as proof that she had no reason to feel so bad. She should be grateful, she contended.

Just out of high school she married the man that she thought would be able to give her everything she had ever wanted emotion- ally—her knight in shining armor. Unfortunately, as is often the case, the shining armor had only been rented, and by the time Beth and her new husband had reached their first anniversary, she was trapped in an abusive, degrading, and humiliating marriage. She focused all of her energy on her children in the years to come, but by the time the youngest had reached adolescence, she was reminded that with all of her children gone, she would once again be alone with her husband. It was around that time that she attended my workshop.

Here is what I *believe* about Beth: She is no different from any of the rest of us in that she must accept responsibility for herself. She would never argue that point. She has certainly been victimized all of her life, but she doesn't have to remain a victim. And yet she remains almost completely paralyzed emotionally. There was a brief time in the midst of her therapy when she did take charge of her life long enough to divorce her husband, but she soon returned to the familiar paralysis.

I believe Beth to be a strong person, but a strong person who has given up on herself and the potential of the world around her. And I believe Beth's paralysis can be explained by remembering the very first word she ever said to me in that workshop many years ago: "Nothing." *What do you believe in? Nothing.*

Beth feels no purpose in her life. According to her, her life is completely pointless. The times when she has considered there might be some point to it all, it seemed to her to be a highly negative point—like the sun is going to come up in the morning, but only to bring one more day of pointlessness. (These are my reflections, not Beth's, so I can't know if she would agree.)

Beth's story is about depression, and it is about the absence of meaning, and it is about self-absorption. That's what depression and meaninglessness will do to us: send us spiraling into ourselves, where we become so tangled in the negative thinking and resulting feelings of despair that we mistake our miserable condition for all of reality. From that dark place, where we can't see a hand in front of our face, we erroneously conclude that this is what life is and all that life can be. It is from this place of pitch darkness that so many people go beyond giving up—they quit.

I don't believe that it is the depression that kills these people. It is something more specific than that—*the absence of meaning kills them.*

Responding

Consider a time in your life when you felt separated from meaning, a time when there was no quality to your life. What were your thoughts about yourself? About the world around you? About the specific people in your life?

Remember a time when someone you cared about felt separated from meaning. What did you feel? What did you say? What did you want that person to understand?

Blocking Purpose:
What's Stopping You?

My faithful *Dictionary of Word Origins* tells me that the word "purpose" can be traced back to the Latin word *proponere*, which means "put forward," or "declare" (Ayto 1990). I have always liked the word "declaration." It is a powerful word: There is no way really to make a declaration timidly. The sentence, "She ambivalently declared her position," doesn't make much sense. I'll bet that America's founding fathers never even considered calling the *Declaration of Independence* the *Proposal of Independence*.

Sometimes I suggest to my clients that they write their own *declarations of independence*. "Declare your independence from your mother and father," I recently told a thirty-two-year-old woman who struggles to see herself as an adult because she continues to yield to their *decisions* for her *life*. I ask my *Self-Forgiveness* Workshop participants to write a declaration of independence from their Should Monsters (inner critics). Once, I even had a client who had become excessively analytical and "therapy-minded" write a declaration of independence from therapy. Like many of us, he had discovered the comfort and safety of sitting in therapy "processing" his problems rather than taking the actions necessary to solve them.

Declaring our independence is a powerful way of stepping into an unknown that we each must face and that we all reasonably fear. Declaring our independence is about declaring ourselves as individuals who are worth—and even require—such a declaration. Without such a declaration, we can only guess (at best) about purpose in our lives.

Beth was able to declare her independence from an abusive husband by getting a divorce, but she believed that the fact that she spent over twenty-five years in that marriage is evidence of her weakness and unworthiness. She has not come much closer to declaring her independence from those ever-present, self-condemning beliefs.

My bottom-line request to Beth has always been, "Don't quit, don't give up now, rest when you must, but always get back up and go again, even when you can't imagine that you have it in you." This may sound discouraging—and it is—but it is realistic in that most of our struggles in life will not fit into nice neat packages. Sometimes what we need more than anything is to declare independence from the internal message that tells us to give up.

My best advice here—and this comes from personal and professional experience—is that when we don't quit, when we refuse to give up on ourselves, we may feel bad at the end of the day, but our self-respect can be intact. Recently, I asked a client at the beginning of a session, "How are you doing?" His response was simple and brilliant. "Are you asking how I am *doing*, or how am I *feeling?* Because I think I am *doing* very well [meaning that he was remaining determined to do what he needed to do to take good care of himself], and I am *feeling* like crap." When we're learning to take responsibility for ourselves, this is one of those *darker before the dawn* times.

"Game over," your inner message may flash. "No way!" you must respond.

Power and Purpose

It is important to know that declaring your independence from anyone or anything is a beginning, not an end. It is a strong statement of determined intent, not a guarantee of outcome. If you're serious about declaring independence, you must thumb your nose at self-defeating, self-hateful beliefs and messages, and you must be willing to take the big risk of claiming your personal power sometimes long before you believe for certain that you even have that kind of power. It is the sense of purpose that fuels the declaration. For instance:

- With a belief in the importance of commitment in his marriage, a man with a history of leaving relationships when the going gets tough declares. "When the temptation to run shows up in my relationship with my wife, I will face that temptation directly and do whatever it takes for me to say no to it."

- A woman who has been taught that she had better settle for what she can get in life declares: "I will pursue what I want in my life, and I won't let old, outdated, false beliefs about myself stop me."

Hiding Out

I recently attended a meeting with a colleague of mine who works in a local hospital. Her office is set deep within a rather large building, and there are no windows to the outside. When I emerged from the hospital, I discovered that a tornado had touched down only a short distance from the hospital, and even a shorter distance from my office. There was considerable damage, but my colleague and I had remained, for the duration of our meeting, oblivious to the threat of severe weather.

Living as a hostage to self-condemning, fatalistic thinking is like being in that office set deep within the building, with no windows to the outside. Beth remains completely cut off from "the external weather conditions." She is trapped in self-absorption and without any sense of her relationship to the outside world, without a connection to any sense of purpose.

To make that connection, we must first make our declaration. We must stand up, walk out of that room with no windows and out of the building that may have protected us, but also left us cut off from the rest of the world.

Self-Denial

Purpose begins with a declaration of your own significance. If you are to be fully responsible for your happiness, you cannot deny that you matter and that you have contributions to make. When you deny your individual significance, you are hiding behind your low self-esteem. You won't do yourself or anyone else any good hiding out in your own private hell.

Judy was a client who had a hard time valuing the quality of life. She was in my office only at the insistence of her two best friends. In a certain way, Judy seemed strong and confident, but in actuality it was life's pointlessness that she was so sure of. She was not at all curious about what I had to offer. She was finished, and because she cared about her two friends, I was one more piece of red tape she had to contend with in order to wrap things up on planet earth.

Judy's plans were interrupted when I asked her if there had ever been a time when she felt like she belonged here on earth with the rest of us. When I asked her that simple question, she looked straight at me with hate in her eyes. Clearly, Judy didn't want to go where that question took her. She told me that there had never been such a time, but she and I both knew that she had blown it. She had accidentally revealed, and I had recognized, a vulnerability in her armor of meaninglessness. Judy had lost something very important to her. I knew that she must have experienced something that hurt her so deeply that she had decided not to go on.

Judy told me later that she wouldn't have come back for a second session had she not promised her two friends that she would attend at least six sessions. But she did return, and by the third session she told me her secret. She had married when she was eighteen her husband had been an alcoholic with a violent temper. It took her until her twenty-ninth birthday, but on that day she gave herself the gift of filing for divorce. Her husband would predictably react in a rage when the papers were served, so Judy's younger brother, Rob, was flying in to stay with his sister for a few days, to celebrate her birthday and her freedom. They had always been close and had always protected each other. This time Judy would be powerless to protect her baby brother. He died along with more than 200 other passengers when his plane malfunctioned and crashed on takeoff.

"It's simple," Judy told me. "Rob would be alive today if he had not been my brother or if I had had the guts to get out of that godforsaken marriage years before, like I should have. I'm a wimp, and because of that, Rob is dead."

For the next couple of sessions, we talked about her brother, Rob. He was four years younger than Bonnie—he was twenty-five when he died. Their father had been particularly hard on Rob, especially during some pretty rebellious adolescent years, but he had "survived his adolescence with flying colors," Judy told me with a pride in her voice that surprised me. Previously she had spoken only in a deadened monotone.

"He had graduated with a degree in business a year before the crash, and he was practically engaged to his girlfriend, Cynthia," Judy said. "Rob had always been moody—I used to call him "Grim" when he was feeling down, and it made him laugh a little—but I think he was feeling better. At least he would have had a chance, if. . . ." Bonnie's voice faded away to nothing.

If he hadn't been your brother," I completed her sentence.

Judy nodded.

"Maybe I should call you Grim," I told her.

When Judy looked at me, the hate was gone, and the pain was front and center.

Self-Indictment

Beth had grown up without a positive sense of herself and her place in the world. Judy's marriage had buried most of her sense of purpose, but that had begun to reemerge by the time she decided to divorce her husband. When her brother died, Judy decided quickly that she was to blame for Rob's death and that she deserved the harshest of punishments for her crime. Beth is still in need of something she has never before known. Judy had stripped herself of a sense of purpose that she had tenuously held onto until her twenty-ninth birthday.

Many of us have made similar decisions, passing judgments on ourselves or accepting judgments from others. These decisions cut us off from the meaning that is required if we are to live fulfilling and responsible lives. No matter how strongly we may feel the guilt of our pasts or the pervasive shame of the present, it is never noble to give up on pursuing purpose in our lives.

Responding

In the past, what are the ways you have cut yourself off from a sense of purpose?

Are there ways in which you are denying or blocking purpose in your life now?

A Common Purpose

A friend of mine, Parker, divides life purposes into two categories: *personal* and *communal*. She says that our communal purpose is the way that we can serve the world (our community) and that our personal purpose is that which must be resolved (personally) before we can effectively enact our communal purpose.

For instance, her communal purpose is as a teacher. She will be increasingly effective in that role as she competently resolves the individual chores associated with her personal purpose of becoming more fully responsible for herself. Specifically for Parker, those chores have to do with commitment in relationships and with financial responsibility.

Whether or not you choose to believe that Parker's model has any objective credibility, I think it is a useful way to think of purpose as a sort of organizing principle in our lives. To be a responsible person you need to work from the inside out, first accepting full responsibility for yourself and then interacting productively with the world around you.

Responding

Consider your own life in terms of personal and communal purposes.

What do you know (or suspect) about your communal purpose?

How has your awareness of communal purpose changed through the years?

What are some of the personal challenges that you believe still need to be resolved in your life?

9

Courage

Overcoming Your Circumstances

The now classic definition of courage is "going on in spite of fear," as distinguished from "the absence of fear." It seems clear to me that as vulnerable, imperfect human beings, in our travels toward ever-increasing personal responsibility, we will predictably be accompanied by fear. Since fear will be coming along whether we like it or not, we had better pack plenty of courage.

The fifteenth-century French philosopher and writer Francois La Rochefocauld said, "Perfect courage means doing unwitnessed what we would be capable of with the world looking on" (1993). I think that is a wonderful measure of our courage.

We usually think of courage in terms of the courageous act: the brave man or woman who rushes into a burning house and emerges with the tiny kitten that was trapped inside, the woman who volunteers for a bone marrow transplant to save someone she has never met, or the man who stands by his principles knowing that he will likely lose his job for doing so.

For people of my generation—and I hope for generations to come—Rosa Parks is the epitome of courage. Ms. Parks can be celebrated for her courageous act of refusing to surrender her seat on a bus because of the color of her skin those many years ago. Yet when we read and listen to what this woman had to say, it becomes apparent that we remember her for one courageous moment from a life that she lived with courage. Rosa Parks has shown us what unrelenting, remarkable courage is like. What she did that day in Montgomery, Alabama, she did without knowing that the world would be looking on. Her courage is synonymous with her "being"; it would be impossible to separate the two. That courageous being has created an increased awareness and change that is still in motion today.

It's not difficult to find role models for courage. I think often of Viktor Frankl, the Austrian psychiatrist who wrote of his experiences in a Nazi death camp during World War II (Frankl 1992), and of Arnold Beisser, M.D., who has written hundreds of articles, contributions for books, as well as best-selling books, in spite of the fact that he has spent the vast majority of his life on life support systems, unable to breath on his own, completely paralyzed except for some of his face and neck muscles, and a small portion of his right hand (Beisser 1990).

Since the accident that paralyzed him, the actor/director Christopher Reeve has been an inspiration for many people with severe physical incapacities. But you don't have to be physically handicapped to be moved by his—and his family's—courage. The way Mr. Reeve so fully lives his life while inhabiting a nearly motionless body is an inspiration for us all.

I heard an interview with Christopher Reeve on the show "20/20," in which he said that if someone were to have asked him (prior to his accident) how he would handle such a tragedy, he would have told them that he would not be able to handle it—that he would not want to live in such a circumstance. Thankfully for him, and for us all, he would have been wrong in his prophecy. Mr. Reeve explained the difference between what he would have thought himself capable of and the reality of his situation by saying simply that we cannot know what we are capable of until we are faced with the circumstances. Here again, the lesson is that true courage emerges not from rational thought, but from the center of our very being. Courage is much more a matter of *who we are* than it is *what we do*.

A Deeper Choice:
Facing Your Fears

"If courage is who we are and not what we do, how can you say that courage is a choice?" The question came during a portion of a talk I gave not long ago. A tough question, but I had an answer.

Responding

Makes some notes about people who have inspired you with their courage

What is it about their spirit that impresses you?

Do you strive for any of these characteristics?

"I suppose this is one of those subjective matters that depends on the individual's personal belief system, and I can only speak from my perspective," I began my response.

"I believe that who we are is a *matter of choice*—or more accurately, it's a matter of many choices. Certainly there are many things in life—most things in life, in fact—that we do not control, and these things can have a tremendous effect on us but they do not determine who we are. It is not *what* happens to us but how we choose to *respond* to what happens that will ultimately determine who we are." Sometimes choosing to challenge the things you cannot control is a courageous act that helps you to earn your own respect.

Who You Are

Someone might fuel this discussion by saying that what happens to us will determine how we will respond, and therefore, in our response, our being is already determined, and so forth. I'm sure that we could become hopelessly lost in the rhetoric of such an esoteric subject. Even now, I can feel myself drawn in by the temptation to recreationally argue both sides of this philosophical debate. However, what is more important than the argument is *the idea of living as if* we always have a choice about who we are. After all, if you live *as if* you have that choice, how can it not be true? You may not choose the circumstances that come your way, but your decisions about what you will do form who you are. For example, Christopher Reeve *chose* to live after his accident and then to teach our society about what it means to be a quadraplegic. He didn't "choose" to be courageous, but the decisions he made about how to respond to his circumstances created a courageous man.

In some ways courage is not a choice that we make in the moment we are faced with our challenge. If we believe, as Christopher Reeve tells us, that we may not know what courage we possess until we are tossed into the deep end of the pool, and if we see in the examples of Mr. Reeve as well as Viktor Frankl, Arnold Beisser, and Rosa Parks that courage and being are inseparable, then we must conclude that whatever courage resides in each of us is the direct consequence of the decisions we have made and the lives we have led up to this very point in time. In other words, courage is a part of who we are that needs to be developed over time; we cannot count on waiting to the last minute to whip up a little courage.

Here is one more of life's many paradoxes: If you perceive yourself as courageous, you probably are not.

Heroes never see themselves as brave; they are just doing what needs to be done. They are being simply who they are due to the choices they have made thus far and acting out of that being.

Learning from the Courageous

Describing how to become courageous is beyond my abilities as a psychotherapist, teacher, and author. And I would have some serious doubts about anyone claiming to possess such a formula. But even if there is no step-by-step plan for insuring our courage, we can learn *about* courage, and the best way I know of to do this is by paying attention to the people around us whom we see as courageous. Obvious teachers are the highly visible and famous, discussed previously. But there are many more: they come in all shapes, sizes, colors, and ages. We just have to *pay attention*.

Sometimes I work with clients who are seriously or even terminally ill. These people are always my teachers, often through their example, and also by virtue of the simple fact that facing their mortality catapults me into facing my own. There may be no greater guide to living a responsible life than evaluating each day from that unknown, future death point, asking the question, "How shall I live this day so that I will feel good about myself when I am looking back from the point of my death?"

I remember Terri, a client with advanced cancer, telling me one day that by paying close attention to some of the others in her cancer support group, especially two who had died in recent months, she felt confident that she "could do it too." Terri added that she understood that sooner or later she would have no choice about whether or not to die but that what she meant was that she now knew that she could face her own death with self-respect and dignity. She described her resulting state of mind as "ready for whatever happens." I call it courage—the ability to keep living her life according to her own choices until that life was over.

About a year later, I attended Terri's funeral, and I remember thinking, "I can do this too." That doesn't make me courageous, certainly not beyond our usual human capacity—facing death is not a unique experience—but it does mean that I am smart. I am smart to be ready and willing to learn from the courageous people that I meet when the paths of our lives cross.

When it comes to learning from the courageous, I think we would all do well to become greedy opportunists. We won't literally be learning how to be courageous. Rather, we will be learning to think and feel straight through our neuroses to the experience of our genuine selves. The more time we spend there, the better.

True courage cannot simply be taught; it must be practiced in our day-to-day lives. And the development of courage cannot be procrastinated. If we want to have courage in the times when we will need it most, we had better be practicing now. "And how do we practice courage?" you might ask. And I might answer: "By being the best selves we can be—one day at a time."

Gratefully, we don't have to be at death's door to learn about or to demonstrate courage. There are examples all around. For instance:

- The businessperson who doesn't allow financial fears to alter her ethics

- The man who objects aloud when someone tells a racist joke

- The physically handicapped child who faces some of the other children's lack of understanding when he goes to school each day

- A woman who leaves an abusive relationship even though she is uncertain about how she will make a living for herself and her children

- A minority person who refuses to allow ignorance and prejudice to stop him from pursuing his dream

---

Responding

Have you known people who have faced the inevitability of death? What did you learn about courage from them?

What is your greatest fear related to your inevitable death?

What other life circumstances can you use to remind you about the importance of courage? What are your simplest reminders?

Our Best Selves

I want to add a word of warning here. Courage comes from our *best selves*, not from our *perfect selves*. Remember that there is no such thing as human perfection, and setting unrealistic expectations based on larger-than-life (such as Hollywood) images is a setup for continued self-critical pain.

Instead, put those grand images of courage into perspective. Our chosen heroes are wonderful symbols for the power and the will to overcome. Be inspired, use the symbolic hero to empower yourself, but don't measure yourself by him or her. The heroics of the movies are our ideals, a part of our culture's mythology. These are stories in which the characters' best selves emerge. Never forget that these characters have an advantage that none of us will ever have in real life: *rewrites*.

Three Steps to Courage

As ordinary human beings, without the benefit of rewrites, it helps to have a tangible plan for activating our best selves. Here is a simple but highly effective technique to employ anytime you are feeling stuck and need that little (or big) additional shot of courage. It's called the *Triple A Technique*.

- **Acknowledge.** First, *inventory your external circumstance and your internal condition*. Be realistic about whatever challenge or problem you're facing, and be honest with yourself about any feelings of shame or fear that may be tempting you to look the other way to avoid facing your impasse.

- **Accept.** This second step is often misunderstood. To accept that things are as they are does not mean that you like them that way or that you agree with their being that way. Acceptance simply means that you recognize the reality that you are facing now. For instance, if you are afraid and refuse to accept the reality of that emotional state, you are only going to create a greater emotional "stuckness" because you will be in danger of feeling ashamed of your fear. The first step to changing something is to accept that *it is as it is*.

- **Act.** Give yourself credit: The first two steps of this technique require courage. But you must not stop there. The third and most crucial step to this plan is *taking action*, somehow acting on your current circumstances in an effort to bring about the changes you desire.

The Plan at Work

Robin didn't have any trouble with step one (**Acknowledge**). She had worked for the company she was with for close to eight years, and although she had learned a lot there, she hated working there now, and she had for at least a solid year. She also acknowledged that her clear dissatisfaction was clouded by her fears—that if she quit her job, she would learn that she was unemployable anywhere else, that she would realize later that she had not been *that* dissatisfied with the job, and that she would have to relocate somewhere she did not like to make a living.

In her group therapy sessions, Robin struggled with the second step (**Accept**) of the *Triple A Technique*. She didn't want to admit how afraid she was. Instead, she would swing from one extreme to the other—feeling confident and excited one minute and discouraged, negative, and fearful in the next. The group helped her to see that being afraid was completely understandable and that only when she could fully accept her fears would she be free to move on to step three: **Act**.

With the other group therapy members as her unofficial consultants, Robin began to take steps toward leaving her job and creating a small agency of her own. By paying attention to her dissatisfaction *and* her fears, she was able to make and follow through with a plan that was proactive but not impulsive. One evening she described to the group her history of swinging back and forth between blind leaps into the unknown and paralysis in the face of any dissatisfaction. It was easy to see how one extreme perpetuated the other. For Robin, true courage was as much about being cautious and realistic as it was about taking chances. Ultimately, her courage led her to carefully considered plans to leave her job and to begin her new business.

Similarly, for many of us, courage is what leads us to take responsible care of ourselves inside and out.

Responding

Who are your symbolic or mythical heroes (they might be from the movies, literature, history, or your own life)? What do your heroes teach you?

As an ordinary human being, apply the *Triple A Technique* to a dissatisfaction in your life.

Getting Unstuck: Free Yourself from Old Circumstances

JoAnn had had quite a lot of therapy by the time she sat in my office. She had grown from those experiences, but she said that she still felt "stranded in limbo."

JoAnn's life had been a strange mix of wonderful and terrible. She had grown up in an affluent home; she had an older sister, and their parents, by all accounts, loved their two daughters very much. JoAnn's father was the classic head of the house, and he made no bones about who made the decisions for the family. He was not, according to JoAnn, physically or verbally abusive, but he definitely dominated his wife, JoAnn's mother. JoAnn's childhood life was filled with activities, good friends, and even regular "family time," dictated by Dad. Her mother was a busy, active woman, but (as JoAnn later identified in therapy) she seemed anxious, constantly on edge, waiting for the "other shoe" to drop. From the outside, JoAnn had the ideal life. And so JoAnn thought as well. "We *were* the perfect family," JoAnn told me. "That is exactly what I thought for a very long time, and that certainly was the way Mom and Dad wanted us to think."

By the time JoAnn was in high school, she had a well-developed streak of angry rebellion, all of it pointed directly at her mother. "I was furious with her," JoAnn said. The older I got, the more independence I wanted, the more of a pain in the ass Mom became. She was constantly getting in my way. I never blew up at her but I was constantly boiling, ready to blow."

JoAnn's relationship with her dad was different. For one thing, it was more distant. He worked a lot and therefore was not home all that much, and even when he was around, JoAnn's descriptions of her dad indicated that he was fairly inept when it came to emotional connection. Her father's way of showing his love was to take care of JoAnn's every need. She always had money (or Dad's credit card) for clothes, she took trips with her friends, and she had a brand-new Mustang convertible by the time she got her driver's license. While JoAnn at times felt like she hated her mother, she saw herself as "Daddy's little girl," even though she had to imagine any emotional fulfillment.

As a young adult, JoAnn was doing pretty well. She attended college at a prominent local university, enjoyed good friends, and she dated a man a few years older who had recently graduated from the same university. Toward the end of JoAnn's second year of college, her best friend committed suicide by running her car off a bridge on the outskirts of town. She had left notes for her parents, her boy-friend, and for JoAnn.

JoAnn, who had no preparation, experience, or support for deal-ing with trauma, was devastated, and she would remain so for years to come. More than twenty years later, JoAnn sat in my office twice a week in hopes of finding her way out of the limbo that she had entered when her good friend had died. She felt that a significant part of herself had died with her friend. "After a couple of months, to everyone's relief, I began to act normal—almost like nothing had hap-pened," she told me. "From there on, I was just going through the motions."

JoAnn married her boyfriend during her senior year, and after about one year of relative normalcy, he became delusional and abu-sive, virtually holding her hostage. "There were times when I thought about getting out," she said, "but mostly I just didn't give a damn. I was like a robot. I just took care of Peter. I did what he said, most of the time—like not going anywhere with my friends.

"My parents were happy. They liked Peter, and of course, he was his charming self whenever they were around. The one time I did call them for help was one of the nights Peter was waving his pis-tols around. That was not so unusual; I had adjusted to his drunken terrorism. But this was the only night that he had ever fired a shot. And he had fired that shot right through the door into our bedroom where I had—as usual—retreated and locked the door." JoAnn might have been responding like a robot, but thankfully, she was still pro-grammed with survival skills.

"I didn't tell my folks everything. I probably told them that Peter was drunk and upset, that I was scared, and asked if they would come over. I'm not sure how much they already knew about how out of control things were for Peter and me, but I'm pretty sure they knew some of it. They were, and still are, masters at pretending that something is not happening if it doesn't fit in with their plans."

"Did they come over?" I asked.

"Yes, they came. By the time they got there, Peter was the one locked in the bedroom—with a bottle of tequila probably. Mom helped me to pack a bag, and Dad paced around the house. I don't think he ever said a word."

"What about the gunshot? Did you tell them about the gun-shot?"

"No. I think I had mentioned that he had his gun out when I called them, but that would have been about all I would have said."

"So neither your Dad nor your Mom said anything to Peter that night?" I asked. I was feeling outraged that her parents had not made a more proactive effort to protect their daughter. "And neither of them knew about the gunshot?"

JoAnn paused. She didn't want to tell this part. "No, I think my dad knew Peter's gun had been fired. You could still kind of smell the powder. Dad had paced back into the hallway near our bedroom at least three or four times. It would be pretty difficult to not see the hole in the door."

"He never asked you about it? Not even later?"

"No, never."

"But they did take you home with them?"

"Yes," JoAnn said, "I went home with them that night. I was exhausted."

"Even the robot was exhausted?"

She smiled. "Yes, Thom, robots get tired too. Anyway, I slept until late into the next afternoon. When I woke up and went into the kitchen, there were two dozen roses beautifully arranged in a crystal vase. I knew who had sent them—it was one more I'm sorry, sweetheart, I'll never do that again, but by the way, you did sort of provoke me, you know . . ."

I needed clarification. "Do you mean that you knew who sent the roses and *you knew who had arranged them?"*

"I mean that I knew that my mother had arranged the roses in the vase. It was one of her vases. She was true to form. As I sat in the kitchen eating lunch, Mom sat with me, talking in her soft, little mom voice, saying how good it was that Peter could admit he was wrong and apologize, and how much she knew he loved me."

I was astounded. "You mean to tell me that she was going to send you back in there?"

"That wasn't surprising," JoAnn said. "You have to remember that this was a good fourteen hours after the fact. Mom had had plenty of time to revise the story to fit her own comfort level. In her mind, by then, nothing really bad had happened. A little spat, she would probably call it. Everything was back to normal."

"Yeah, normal. Real normal." I just shook my head.

JoAnn did pull free of that marriage or, more accurately, that hostage situation. A male friend of hers from college had moved back to town. He saw what was going on, began to ask questions, and eventually he talked her through the divorce. He was married, with a family, with no romantic interest in JoAnn. He was just a good friend, and like many of JoAnn's friends, he began to call less and less as she stopped returning phone calls. As JoAnn and I later characterized it, she was like a long-term prisoner who was paroled and didn't know how to handle the freedom.

Even though JoAnn's childhood was far from horrendous, she still had little say in the decisions that affected her own life. Her father provided for her well, but he did so always on his terms, based on what he wanted for JoAnn. I remember asking JoAnn one day if she could remember either one of her parents expressing curiosity about what she thought or felt about something. She listened to my question, thought about it for a moment, and then said flatly, "No."

With her father making all of the decisions and her mother condoning this, JoAnn married a man who played the role of both parents—to an extreme. Sadly, once her friend helped urge her out of the marriage, JoAnn became a self-contained dysfunctional family. Even though she got out of her marriage, JoAnn had still not confronted her feelings of low self-worth. She still needed to face the truth about her family and move beyond their bad choices. At first, she held herself hostage still, isolating in herself at home and criticizing herself constantly, telling herself that whatever she thought or felt must be wrong, crazy, or somehow defective. And don't forget: A part of JoAnn had not been seen since her friend drove off the bridge.

JoAnn had worked with two therapists previously and had benefited from both. She was referred to me by one of those therapists, who recognized how stuck JoAnn was feeling and thought a little change might be good for her client. Specifically, the therapist had suggested to JoAnn that she work with a male therapist, which she had not done before. The therapist thought that JoAnn's problem—long-term limbo—might be just up my alley.

Moving On

The essence of JoAnn's and my work together was (1) to compile JoAnn's history in the context of her "stuckness," (2) to determine as specifically as we could what JoAnn wanted from her therapy experience and what she believed was possible, and (3) to become as creative as we needed to be in order to accomplish what JoAnn wanted her future to be like.

Much of our work had to do with building up her self-esteem and motivation. The turning point of JoAnn's therapy, however, came down to a question of courage. JoAnn was the product of an overprotected life. This always struck me as ironic when I thought of how angry I had felt at her parents' total lack of protection when JoAnn was in such danger in her marriage. But it was true. She had been shielded from the need—and even her right—to make decisions for herself. Her father made all of her major decisions (from his emotionally distant position), and her mother continually reinforced the idea that JoAnn did not have good judgment—that she wasn't capable of making the *right* decisions. She might have shaken off much of this family baggage if her friend had not killed herself. Just when JoAnn was beginning to experience some personal freedom, she took such a painful hit that it sent her spiraling back into the safety of those familiar family dynamics—thus, her marriage. The familiar, even when it is negative, can be quite comforting.

It was the freshly emerging "Free JoAnn" that she sent flying off that bridge with her friend. With her friend's death, JoAnn experienced what I call the *I-told-you-so-within*. The underlying message of most overprotective families is, "It's not safe out there in the real world. We can't handle it, so we should take refuge in our inadequacies; we invent our own worlds and stay out of the line of fire." The line of fire being otherwise known as *life*. JoAnn had ventured out, and in doing so, she was taking the risks that we all must take to become thinking, capable adults. Unfortunately, she soon lost her best friend, in a particularly horrible way, and from deep inside of JoAnn the family message arose: "I told you so," it said to her. "Now get back in here where you belong."

JoAnn wanted to change. In a little over a year of our regular sessions, she had become clear that no part of her had died with her friend's suicide. That part of her, the "Free JoAnn," had gone into hiding, exiled by the *I-told-you-so* message, but she was not dead. JoAnn was not only not dead, but she was no longer deadened. The robot was gone. I remember in particular a group session in which JoAnn was crying, experiencing some very painful feelings. Another woman in the group, remembering that JoAnn's goal was to "be back among the living," took JoAnn's hand, offered her a box of tissues, and said, "Welcome back."

JoAnn was just beginning to learn how to feel and respond in her first year of college, and when her friend committed suicide, she came rushing back into the safety of a controlled situation. Before she knew it, she was trapped again.

More than twenty years later, JoAnn began where she had left off. She put her house on the market. She told me that she needed to get rid of her "hideout." She had always lived in Nashville, and she discovered something she had previously known only vaguely: that she had always wanted to move away, to leave her home town. Maybe what she really longed for, I suggested, was to finally make her own decisions. She decided to rent a place in Southern California, with plans to buy a home if she liked living there as much as she thought she would.

During the preceding months, JoAnn had begun to experiment with being increasingly honest with her friends and family. As it is with learning anything new, she was clumsy at first—being either too timid or too aggressive at times. But she was getting the feel of it. Some of her friends who depended on JoAnn to be the same good ole malleable JoAnn either expressed their disapproval or just faded away. Other friends were elated to see their friend so alive; they celebrated. Her parents and her sister were at times perplexed and at times hurt, but before long, there seemed to be some degree of acceptance that JoAnn was going to be different. They didn't necessarily understand it, but they seemed to be able to respect it.

JoAnn's confidence did not shoot up over night. She still felt the pull of the old safe, controlling dynamics. But her courage remained, and with it, the knowledge that going out into the world—or not—was a choice, a choice that JoAnn and every one of us has to make every day. And when we make the choice to make self-responsible choices, we cannot afford to wait for reassurance that will make the fear go away. If the fear is there, it's there—usually in the form of a big threat, something like, "You'll be sorry if you go through that door. You will fall flat on your face, and there will be no one there to pick you up."

When any of us hear and feel those threats, there are no reassurances to make the fear go away. The only real reassurance is to look the threat square in the eye, fully aware of the fear provoked by the threat, and say, "I am willing to risk it. Maybe I will fall, and maybe I will not. If I do, I am committed to getting back up again," to the big bad threat. We remember the old adage that says *If I fall down sixteen times, I will get up seventeen.* And then we walk right past the mean old threat. To do otherwise would be to make the choice of storing away a part of life.

A year after she moved to California, JoAnn bought a house in San Diego. That was about two years ago. JoAnn is currently considering a move back to Nashville. She says that she misses her friends here, that she wants to be nearer her parents as they are growing older, and that she may have had enough sun and surf. What JoAnn decides and where she decides to live is inconsequential. What is important is that she is doing the choosing. She is making the choices and taking the risks. That's life; that's courage.

The Will to Risk

Imagine that you are sitting in the middle of a room. The room has a floor and a ceiling, and it has four walls, but there are no windows or doors. Now imagine that you were born into this room, and it is all you have ever known. This room is your universe, this is what you *know.*

Now, imagine that you look up one day, and there right in the middle of one of the walls is a door. It is closed, so you don't know what is on the other side, but you know that this is definitely an opening that will lead you out of your room. What do you think? What do you feel? What do you do?

Responding

Consider the visualization above. Make some notes about what you see, hear, and feel in response.

The Courage to Look Inward

It takes courage to step out into a world full of risks as JoAnn has done. The choice that she has made and that we all must make is between *hiding out* and *stepping out*. It can be encouraging to say that the joys that we encounter are well worth the risk of pain. Such a statement from others who have taken the risk before us will have great value in its supportiveness, and in that it gives us hope. *If you have done this, then so might I.* But ultimately there is no guarantee that stepping into the experience of life will be worth the risk. I can say that *I would rather go down with the ship than not to sail at all,* but I cannot know that for you.

Responding

What are some risks you feel you're ready to face that you've been avoiding for a while?

How do you feel about the risks? Be sure to allow yourself more than one feeling.

The extent of your involvement with the direction of your life is a matter of choice. Much of what will happen to you in this life will result from your choices. However, what actually happens is still beyond your choice or control. As you consider "stepping out," the question you need to ask yourself is this: *Am I prepared to remain in charge of my decisions or responses even in the event of a complete loss of control?* If you answer "yes" to this question, *make a commitment to yourself that you will accept full responsibility for the choices that will need to be made, that as the captain of the ship, you will not abandon the bridge even in the roughest of waters.*

Answering "yes" also requires a commitment to look inward for the lessons of responsibility—that is, really look inside and face those fears that have been tucked away. It is my experience—and that of many others I have talked with—that the willingness to look inside yourself with clarity and honesty is the greatest challenge to your courage. To do this work, which calls for a lifelong commitment, you will face the sources of the greatest human anxieties: death, meaninglessness, and condemnation (Tillich 1963).

Another obstacle that may come up when you begin to look inward is believing *self-hate* and *self-condemnation* to be the equivalent of *self-responsibility*. Nothing could be further from the truth. I wrote *The Self-Forgiveness Handbook* to make this very point:

> *If we truly desire to be self-responsible people, we must be willing and able to sort through the baggage we all carry, learning to let go of self-blame for those things we had no control over and learning to forgive ourselves for the mistakes we have made along the way.*

Genuine, contentious self-forgiveness is not self-indulgence, and it isn't the practice of making excuses for ourselves. To forgive ourselves is to *make sure we learn the lessons, then to let go of the excess baggage, and then to move on.* I like to think of it as *traveling light.*

10

Humility

You're Not Alone

"What are you most afraid of?" she asked. I don't remember how we got on the subject of fear, but this was psychotherapy after all.

I took the question in, repeated it to myself: *What am I most afraid of?* My answer came quickly, and it surprised me. "Being *ordinary*. That's my greatest fear."

Linda, my therapist those many years ago, did not seem surprised by my answer. "Describe 'ordinary' to me," she said.

"Ordinary," I said as if I were in a spelling bee, "my idea of ordinary is losing all sense of individuality. Like getting up in the morning, going to work in a pin-striped suit, with the standard maroon necktie, with a briefcase like everyone else's, with a haircut that is indistinguishable from my fellow residents in hell, to a day that is dedicated to meeting somebody else's agenda that I have no personal interest in. And at the end of my day that never belonged to me in the first place, I would go to sleep so that I could get up the next morning and do it all over again."

What I have discovered since that therapy session many years ago is that my fear of being ordinary is not at all unique; you might even say it's quite ordinary. Each of us may have a different picture of what it means to be ordinary, but most of us will have, in one form or another, some fear of blending into the background of life, a fear that we might never distinguish ourselves from the masses.

The Value of Ordinary: The Universality Inherent in Our Human Experiences

I now consider it my challenge to make peace with my own aspects of ordinariness. I have learned that without it, I am alone—and by my own making. To acknowledge the many ways in which we are all ordinary does not negate our individuality; in fact, it strengthens it.

Acknowledging how we are often ordinary and in many ways like everyone else is the experience of *humility*. Humility is the *knowledge of our sameness, of our connection to other individuals and to community at its many levels, from familial to global*. Humility is characterized by an awareness of who we are (as opposed to what we can do), and in this way, humility is an important part of developing realistic and positive self-esteem. We all, for example, experience the following:

- Love
- Hate
- Fear
- Joy
- Pain
- Regret
- Excitement
- Disappointment

Abraham Lincoln is an excellent example of a man who certainly distinguished himself from his peers, a man of many qualities that were, to say the least, extraordinary; but by all we know of this great man, he appears to have perceived himself in quite ordinary terms. It might even be said that a significant part of Lincoln's greatness emanated from his refusal to think of himself as different from others.

Humility is often erroneously associated with the experience of being *less than* others and is equated with low self-esteem. However, to feel less good or less worthy than another is an experience of *separation*, not connection. There is a big difference between what we call *humiliation* and *humility*. (We will discuss humiliation soon.)

Humility, as we will see in this chapter, can be evasive, confusing, and even tricky, but one thing is for sure: *Humility is the bedrock of personal responsibility.*

Responding

What are your associations with the word *humility*? How are you ordinary?

Do you have role models for humility? (They can be anyone from Ghandi to your grandmother.)

Blocks to True Humility

Try to strike a balance between "too much humble pie" and a true awareness that we are all feeling a similar range of emotions just by being human. We sometimes believe that if we can (1) just keep our egos in check, or better yet, (2) we can regularly remind ourselves of our flaws, or (3) if we can consistently beat the hell out of ourselves, we will remain humble. I don't think so. Remember, humility is about connection and celebration of our sameness. Each of these three tendencies is still about the individual and is more likely to contribute to further self-absorption than to a sense of connection.

It is not always easy to agree about what genuine humility is and, more important, how to get there. In an effort to clear the path, I have defined what I consider to be the four major obstacles that will come between you and genuine humility. They are as follows: *mixed messages, humiliation, false humility*, and *grandiose humility*. Let's look at each of these more closely.

Mixed Messages

We live in a culture that tells us to blend with the scenery *and* to muscle our way to the top so that we can stand apart from our peers. There is no way that anyone can adequately satisfy an instruction that calls for conformity and rebellion simultaneously. And unfortunately, this double message doesn't usually mean that there is no way to get it wrong, but instead that there is no way to get it right. When I choose to conform, remaining in the background, I feel criticized for being weak, lazy, or inept. When I choose to pull away from the crowd, showing myself to be unique, I feel criticized for being either arrogant, threatening, or crazy. These confusing contradictions can throw us toward one extreme and then another, far from the commonality of humility.

Criticisms like these have been strengthened by the cultural contradictory messages. Self-criticism is the most powerful and potentially the most debilitating criticism of all. Self-criticism, ironically, is the enemy of humility. The idea is not to think you are of no individual importance, but to realize how much you have in common with everyone in some way or another.

We have grown up in the midst of such double-binding, no win messages as:

- Do what it takes to succeed, but be sure everyone around you is always happy.

- Always take responsibility for yourself, but don't take time to respond to your own needs.

- It is important to excel in whatever you do, but it is selfish and bad to think well of yourself.

These messages, and others like them, can paralyze us. They can cause us to feel insecure and negative about ourselves, but they will not—as many of them are intended—help us to develop a *healthy* sense of humility. These messages are nothing more than the unresolved confusion of one generation being handed down to the next. Perpetuating our sense of separation from one another, confusing us, and debilitating our self-esteem—that is the power of the double-binding mixed messages. If we are to find our way to the humility that I believe is our first nature, we must first find our way through the double-binding messages that unfortunately have become our second nature.

Humiliation

These messages passed from one generation to the next appear to be based on a fear of our own potential. This fear is often ingrained in us by others—for some reason, individuality is usually feared by the group mentality. It often threatens the illusion of safety and order. Think about it, though:

- Exactly what horrible consequence is supposed to befall you if you dare to think well of yourself?

- Who exactly will be destroyed if you don't achieve the impossible task of keeping everyone around you happy and satisfied?

- Are you so powerful in the grand scheme of things that tending to your own business and feeling good about it will cause damage in the world around you?

One more time: I don't think so. The larger message imbedded in the many specific messages is that we cannot be trusted—with positive self-esteem, with success, with happiness. We are imprinted with the belief that our gain will always be someone else's loss or that somehow we will use our gain to inflict injury on others. Ultimately we are taught that to be good we must see ourselves as bad. I am reminded of a quotation from Neitzsche, in my *International Thesaurus of Quotations*:

> *He who despises himself nevertheless esteems himself as a self-despiser.*

This is not descriptive of humility; it is the state of *humiliation*. And no matter how widespread and common the state of humiliation may be, it will not serve to connect us to others. Feeling less than others will only serve to further isolate us.

Hiding Behind False Humility

I learned a while back that if you want to know where someone stands in relation to humility, observe them in a group or community setting. *False humility*, in particular, becomes extremely visible in such a setting.

Clara was a twenty-two-year-old woman participating in my group for bulimic and anorexic women. She had fit in with the other group members almost from the moment of her arrival. She was friendly and funny, and she participated actively in all of the group discussions and activities. Clara was particularly supportive to the other women in the group, always ready and willing to share some of her own recovery failures to demonstrate that they weren't alone in their frustration. She seemed, in fact, to be the epitome of humility.

One evening, however, group members began asking Clara more specific questions about how she was doing. They expressed their concern that while she had been supportive to them, they had not had the chance to return the favor. Clara was noticeably uncomfortable as these tables turned on her, but she began to answer the group's questions once it was apparent that there would be no avoiding it. What emerged was Clara's model for recovery from an eating disorder that was entirely different from what she had been suggesting to and supporting in the other group members.

While she always insisted to the others that there "is no shame" in needing other people's help in their efforts to change, Clara held a different standard for herself. Although she had supported other group members to work with a qualified nutritionist in developing an appropriate food plan for their eating-disorder recovery, Clara had consulted a nutritionist once, three years previous, and only at her parents' insistence. She described parts of her own "food plan" that were obviously not within the range of healthy eating and defended her thinking with rationalizations and distortions of the truth. Before the group ended that evening, everyone in the group, including myself, had expressed sincere concern for her. One of the women asked Clara if she would be willing to talk more about her recovery plan in next week's session. Clara agreed, but. . . .

Clara didn't return to the group the following week. Instead, she left a message saying that she felt she had learned a lot from participating in the group, but that now she thought she had gotten all that she could from that setting and had decided to move on.

This is not a story about a woman deceiving a group of other women. False humility is much more about self-deception than it is anything else. I see this same double standard at work in group therapy frequently, and in my weekend retreats. Clara meant what she said in support of the other members of the group; she believed that for them there was "no shame" in needing help to recover from their eating disorders. She simply held herself to a completely different standard. She held herself apart from the others. She missed out on recognizing the *sameness* of herself and the group.

In some ways, we might view this as *negative arrogance*; that is, seeing herself as different from others because she is less worthy. I believe that as a psychological defense, Clara thought herself to be weaker than the other women in her group therapy, and therefore was scared to face the truth because she didn't think she'd be able to really change. I didn't get a chance to ask her, but I am willing to bet that Clara's greatest fear is being ordinary.

Grandiose Humility

A young man named Bart described a relationship problem he was having with his girlfriend to the other members of his therapy group. He was confused; "truly stumped" was his term. Bart asked for help from the group. In response to his request, a couple of group members shared some of their own experiences with similar problems. Then Frank, a man in his fifties, spoke: "God knows that I am probably the most screwed-up person in this room. Surely I am the farthest thing from an expert on the subject of relationships. I should probably keep my mouth shut— but I will tell you what I think about your little dilemma. . . ." And for the next several minutes Frank explained exactly what Bart's problem was and built a long list of things Bart "should" do. The other group members shifted uncomfortably in their chairs until Frank brought his speech to a close. He ended with the phrase, "But what do I know?"

This is an example of *grandiose humility*. Essentially, grandiose humility is *blatant arrogance* covered with a thin layer of *pseudo-humility*. The grandiose humble among us are those who claim to be connected to the masses but who continue to sit in judgment of the rest of us.

Responding

What mixed, double-bind, or contradictory messages are you aware of in your own programming?

What are some instances when you've mistaken the state of humiliation for humility?

What false humility or double standards have you had by which you held yourself to an unrealistic higher standards than you held for others?

Can you think of an example of when you have been grandiosely humble?

Use the information about the four major blocks to humility to increase awareness of yourself, not to assess and judge others. Continue to identify mixed messages in your thinking, distinguish between humility and humiliation, strive to connect to others by holding yourself accountable to the same standards you have for them, and learn to interrupt your own grandiosity so that someone else won't need to.

From Shame to Humility

Humility is not about being in the *one down* position; it's about being on a *level playing field*. It's not about being in a position of unreasonable vulnerability; it's about being in a position of strength. But the strength of humility isn't strength that is wielded over or against anyone or anything else; it's a strength that comes from knowing that we have a place in this world—*that we belong*.

The Pedestal Problem

Dale described his father as the most humble man on earth. Clearly he had tremendous respect for the man who had helped to bring him into this life. Dale had previously been in therapy with me for about a year and a half, but as he sat in my office for this visit, I had not seen him for over two years.

Dale was specific about the reason for making the appointment. He had recently participated in an intensive week-long therapeutic program that focused on family-of-origin learning. He had emerged from the experience with uncharacteristically angry feelings toward his father.

"I've always known that I was angry with my mother," he said, "but until now, I don't think I have ever felt anger toward Dad. I don't like it. Can you make it go away?" The question was intended as a joke, but it revealed something very important: Dale was afraid to be angry with his father. With my help, he would need to discover what was so scary, face it, and then find permission within himself to experience the very normal feeling of anger toward his father.

Since I had worked with Dale before and knew him well, I cut to the chase. "What's so frightening about being angry at your dad?"

Dale listened to my question and said, "I hadn't thought of it as being afraid; I was thinking of it as being angry."

"But which one of those feelings are you experiencing right now . . . right now when we talk about your new anger at your dad?"

"Okay you're right. It's fear."

"So what is so scary about being angry at your dad?" I waited for Dale to respond.

"I don't know," he finally answered. "All I know is that he is a good man, the best man I have ever known, and he doesn't deserve my anger."

"What's the problem with being angry with the best man you've ever known? Your anger doesn't have to bring any harm to him."

Dale looked scared now. "It feels like it will—hurt him, that is."

"So you're afraid that your feelings are going to hurt your father?"

"That's only part of it," Dale said. "It feels bigger than that."

"Well, if it feels bigger than that, then it is bigger than that." I was reminding Dale of some of the therapy work we had done previously about trusting his instincts.

"Oh yeah, right, I remember." Dale smiled.

Again, depending on the positive relationship we had developed in the past, I suggested, "Maybe you're afraid that by acknowledging your anger at your father, you're going to knock him off the pedestal you have him on."

Dale looked perplexed.

"Is that it? Are you afraid of bumping him off the pedestal?" I pressed a little.

"Maybe I need him on that pedestal. Maybe I need to be able to admire him."

"Maybe," I replied, "but maybe you could gain more from the relationship if you did get him off the pedestal. It might be more difficult to have relationships with real, live, flesh-and-blood people, but the reward can be well worth the effort."

A Level Playing Field

What I knew about Dale is that he had struggled long and hard with a pervasive sense of shame, and he probably still did to one degree or another. I also knew that he had never been willing to look too closely at his relationship with his father when we had worked together before.

What Dale and I discovered, over the next six or eight weeks, was that his father had most likely felt a lot of shame throughout his life as well. Outwardly, he was the kind, generous, good-hearted man whom Dale had placed on a pedestal. But inwardly, Dale's father suffered from low self-esteem. He even told Dale and his brother on more than one occasion that he knew he had been a complete failure in life. Dale, of course, knew this not to be so and simply categorized the statement under "More evidence that Dad is the most humble man on earth."

I suggested, and eventually Dale agreed, that he visit his father—who lived some distance away—for the purpose of talking with him about the work he and I had been doing in therapy.

Dale returned from this "therapy field trip" with a new feeling toward his father: *sadness*. During their time together, Dale's dad confirmed that he indeed saw himself as a miserable failure in life. Fortunately, Dale knew better than to try to rescue his father from his lifelong poor self-image. He expressed his feelings of anger with his father. He also told him of many ways he had been positively influenced by him. But as far as Dale could tell, none of what he had said to his father seemed to matter much.

Over the course of the next couple of sessions Dale came to realize that as a child, he had unconsciously chosen to put his father on a pedestal for two excellent reasons: (1) He needed to have a father he could be proud of, and (2) his dad was not particularly capable of having a genuine relationship with his son, because he was so absorbed in his own shame and negativity. When Dale attended the week-long therapeutic program, the truth had been pushed to the surface. Dale began to feel angry at his father for his emotional absence and for having taught Dale (by example) to be *ashamed of himself*, mistaking the *shame* for *humility*.

We were now able to answer the original question of "What's so scary about being angry with your father?" more specifically. Dale knew intuitively that despite the image of his father as strong and patient, he was really quite fragile. Symbolically, Dale feared that his anger would easily destroy the man, that he couldn't stand up to it. Additionally, Dale feared that his own anger at his father's shortcomings would validate his father's view of himself as a failure. Of course, Dale did not want to think of his father in these terms.

Dale and I finished his second series of therapy sessions soon after these realizations. Dale's challenge as we parted this time was to throw out his old definition of humility (*shame*) and begin to build a brand-new definition. Since he had discovered how isolated his father's shame had made him, Dale wanted a definition that would reconnect him to the people in his life. In our last session, Dale told me this: "The humility I am seeking has nothing to do with pedestals or self-imposed prison sentences."

Responding

In what ways have you mistaken shame for humility?

The Strength of Humility

G. K. Chesterton, an English essayist writing in the early part of the twentieth century, wrote, "It is always the secure who are humble" (1988). *Security* and *humility*: These two conditions will always coexist for the fully responsible person. In the deepest sense, for responsible human beings, one of these conditions cannot exist without the other. Let us take a look now at what I have come to consider the three ingredients essential to the creation and maintenance of these interdependent conditions of *security* and *humility*.

Three Essential Ingredients

For the responsible person, humility encompasses three essential ingredients. The ingredients are as follows:

1. **Respect for our imperfection.** This is the basic understanding that we are imperfect human beings and that only when we can accept that *perfection is not a viable option for ourselves or others* will we be in a position to experience peace of mind. Accepting that perfection is not humanly possible doesn't mean that we should give up our efforts to excel in all that we do.

2. **Knowledge of our commonality with others.** This refers again to our being in touch with our *sameness*, how we are alike. It is our connection to all community—from familial to global. Contrary to our fears, acknowledging our commonality with others will not rob us of any of our unique features. In fact, with a strong connection to community, we will each have a sturdy foundation on which to build our individual lives.

3. **Active, genuine contact with others on our common ground.** This is about the congruence discussed in chapter 5. The responsible person doesn't stop at the point of gaining knowledge; the responsible person puts that knowledge into action. In this case, the action is about having genuine relationships with other human beings, in all their imperfection.

Responding

Describe each of the three ingredients as they are working, or as you want them to be working, in your life.

The Paradox

I have a friend who refers to what she calls "God's lousy sense of humor." She is talking about how paradox seems so prevalent in our lives. I don't know if it has anything to do with God's sense of humor, but I am aware of the paradox. For instance, after seeking publishing contracts for seven years, I made a decision to let go entirely of the idea of getting such a contract. I made the solid decision that I would continue to produce my materials through my own small publishing house. Disappointment was behind me; I felt relieved by my decision.

A little over a week later, I received a call from the acquisitions editor for New Harbinger Publications. She had seen one of my press kits and wanted to know if I could write a book for them about self-forgiveness. By the end of the next week, I had signed my first publishing contract. Maybe God's sense of humor is at best a little strange.

There is a similar paradox with humility, and it is this: *If you really want to be special, to make your mark in life, then let go of your need for that specialness.* Seek instead your connection to everyone else, your common ground, and before you know it, you will discover your special place in the larger scheme of it all.

What I once thought of as hell is now an essential part of the foundation for my life: my ordinariness. Won't you join me?

EPILOGUE

Putting It All Together

*The map's in your soul
and the road's in your mind.*

—Dan Fogelberg
"The Wild Places"

*From century to century it has become more and more
evident that knowledge without wisdom produces external and internal self-destruction.*

—Paul Tillich
The Eternal Now

The Lesson

Putting Your Decision Maker to Work

Depending on when you ask me, I might tell you that as a psychotherapist I

- Have the greatest job on earth
- The silliest job on earth
- The easiest job on earth
- The most difficult job on earth
- The most confusing job on earth
- The most fascinating job on earth

I have been known to walk into my associate's office at the end of a really "good" day, plop down on his couch, and say, "Now tell me again, very slowly this time: What is it that we do for a living?"

My fluctuating thoughts and feelings used to scare me. I thought that my lack of certainty was evidence of incompetence. Now I tend to believe quite the opposite. It is the therapist with absolute certainty and total confidence who scares me. I don't want to, and I don't recommend, walking around in constant anxiety and desperate fear of incompetence, but I have learned that a little bit of fear and uncertainty about what I am doing works for me and therefore works for my clients. It keeps me honest. It keeps me awake. And it keeps me ready to learn. If I am not ready, willing, and able to learn as I sit with a new client, I will be treating that client only according to what I know about *other* people. Would you want to be that new client? I wouldn't.

Since we cannot teach what we do not know, in order to teach self-respect to others, I must respect myself. One essential aspect of that self-respect is the acknowledgment of all that I do not know. This acknowledgment, and eventual acceptance, of my "not knowing," rather than being the manifestation of my greatest fears of inadequacy, can become an empowering gift as long as I remain willing and able to transform my ignorance into curiosity.

This Magic, Uncertain Moment

Genuine curiosity is a powerful expression of respect. Curiosity, by definition, is an *admission of a lack of knowledge*. When I am curious about what you have to say, that means that I have not jumped ahead in the conversation (not entirely anyway) to predict or assume what you will say next. That's not easy to do—give it a try.

When we listen to each other with curiosity, when we are willing and able to take turns doing so, when we can surrender our delusional hold on changing the past and controlling the future, we enter into the *present moment*. In this present moment we can make contact with one another—a truly effective relationship can exist, in which I accept responsibility for accurately representing myself and you do the same for yourself. A relationship in such a condition will be balanced, fair, and open. A relationship in such a condition will be capable of productive collaboration, whether it be for the purpose of deciding what movie to see or how to overcome a major obstacle. And a relationship in such a condition exists in a state of uncertainty.

The Challenge

Ironically, it is only when we acknowledge the reality that all things are constantly changing that we have a chance to experience genuine security. I keep a sign posted above a dartboard in my office that says:

Of All Things Impermanent
Hold Nothing Sacred

When I receive a rejection notice from a magazine, newspaper, or book publisher, it goes immediately on the dartboard. That rejection notice becomes my target for the next couple of days. When I receive good news in the mail—*yes, we think you have a great idea and we want to work with you in publishing your project*— that letter goes on the dartboard too. This is not an expression of negativity or a way of minimizing a success. Throwing darts at the good news has become just another part of the celebration, and most of all, it is that tangible reminder to keep my feet planted firmly on the ground. *Of all things impermanent, hold nothing sacred.*

Right Here, Right Now

The best place to be is here and now. It is entirely possible that we are here on planet earth to learn this one, and only this one, lesson. One . . . simple . . . lesson.

It wouldn't be surprising to learn that we have been here through the ages, in pursuit of "the lesson," only to become distracted again and again—distracted not only from learning the lesson, not only from accurately identifying the lesson, but often distracted from even knowing that there is a lesson. "Hey, can I borrow your notes from class?" you ask. I reply: "What class?"

Even on the days when I feel confident that I know what the lesson is, I'm not particularly good at practicing it. My best guess is that who or whatever is in charge of the universe has placed us here along with the one simple lesson, *and* along with the following instructions.

Instructions

Do the best you can. Try not to kick yourself too hard when you can't seem to get it right or when you realize that you forgot to show up for practice.

Take responsibility for your own efforts, and subsequently for your own errors and for your successes. Remember that *responsibility is the key*, not blame. When you take responsibility for yourself, you earn your own respect.

Review *the lesson* once or twice every day, and practice applying it to your life at least that often.

Continued on next page.

The Lesson

In this precise moment, you are *100 percent in charge of your decision making.* In the next moment, the same will be true. And in the next, and the next. Your mission—on the days you decide to accept it—is to focus as much of yourself in this precise moment as you possibly can. Make conscious decisions *from this moment on.* Your decisions can be based on what has gone before and on what you want or need in the future, but you can only decide in *the now,* and you can only act in *the now.*

That's all. Go practice it . . . *now!*

The Seven Components of Personal Responsibility

Here is a brief overview of the seven components.

Component 1: Self-Esteem

It is easy enough to say—and know—that positive self-esteem is an attribute of a healthy person. Two challenges remain for the responsible person: (1) to understand that positive self-esteem is not a luxury, but a necessity, and (2) to learn specifically *how* to develop and maintain positive self-esteem.

Oftentimes, the better we feel about ourselves, the less self-absorbed we become. When we accept the responsibility to identify and meet our own needs for genuine, positive self-esteem, we are in a position to respond with *power, authenticity,* and *compassion,* to the world around us.

Component 2: Congruence

As a society we can say that we share a baseline of common values—*thou shalt not kill,* for example. The readers (and writer) of this book will no doubt share many values in common, but each of us will also have our own unique set of values—*a personal value system that must be explored and defined.*

Although the presence of a strong, evolved value system is certainly a characteristic of a responsible person, there is something that is more telling, and that is the congruence of the person's expressed values with his actions in the world.

If I review a job description and accept a job you have offered me but never, or seldom, show up for work, I will not be valued as a responsible employee. No one will defend me by saying, "Well, he did read the job description, and he really liked it. He said he could definitely do the job."

There are three parts of this second component: (1) becoming conscious of our personal value systems, (2) knowing that once our eyes are open, value systems are built, revised, and maintained according to our choices, and (3) to the very best of our (imperfect) ability, we act in our world according to our expressed value systems.

Component 3: Motivation

Motivation is fuel; it keeps us moving. Without fuel, no matter how wonderful our intentions may be, we will not be acting responsibly. Motivation is both a simple and a complex matter. The responsible person must understand the importance of motivation, but more than that, like a chemist she must know the formula for creating and maintaining motivation. In its simplest terms, that formula is

Desire + Hope = Motivation

The responsible person knows that, like gasoline, dissatisfaction can be used constructively or destructively. Her job is being aware of her dissatisfactions, combining them with hope (in the form of a belief in her own potential for change), and using that mixture to fuel appropriate decisions and actions toward positive change.

Component 4: Power

When we are doing what is required by the first three components, we will become increasingly, and maybe uncomfortably, aware of our power. *The responsible person is a powerful person.* He must accept that power and commit himself to understanding what it means to be responsibly powerful.

This component is the *middle component* of the seven: It is created and increased by the consistent practice of the first three components, and it will be instrumental in the practice of components five, six, and seven. The responsible person is required to accept, protect, understand, harness, and use personal power *for* himself and others, and never against anyone. For most of us, learning to make this distinction will be a life-long project.

Component 5: Purpose

Sometimes experiencing a sense of purpose is as much a matter of faith or trust as it is understanding or knowing. Being aware of purpose—both generally and specifically—is the compass for the responsible person. *With purpose, we maintain direction and orientation.* After enough experience with purpose, even when we feel lost or aimless, we will remember that there is purpose—and that if we can't find it, as long as we don't go into hiding, it will always find us.

Component 6: Courage

Courageous people don't usually experience themselves as brave. The responsible person understands that courage isn't a characteristic that is above and beyond the call of human duty. Courage is a natural part of us all; *the responsible person's task is not to create courage, but to find it within herself and to cultivate it as a part of daily life.* Courage in the humdrum of daily life is the extra nudge, or surge of confidence, that we all need in order to step toward the lessons and challenges that scare us.

Component 7: Humility

Humility is the component of balance for the responsible person. It is the necessary reality check to keep us on track. For the responsible person, humility encompasses three essential ingredients: (1) respect for our imperfection (human-ness), (2) knowledge of our "sameness," our common ground with others, and (3) active, genuine contact with others on that common ground.

Humility is the great connector.

References

Alcoholics Anonymous. 1976. *Alcoholics Anonymous, 3d ed*. New York: Alcoholics Anonymous World Services, Inc.

Auden, W. H. 1966. *Collected Poems*. New York: Vintage Books.

Ayto, John. 1990. *Dictionary of Word Orgins*. New York: Arcade Publishing.

Bach, Richard. 1977. *Illusions*. New York: Delacorte Press.

Bandler, Richard, and John Grinder. 1981. *Frogs into Princes: Neuro Linguistic Programming*. Moab, Utah: Real People Press.

Beattie, Melody. 1997. *Stop Being Mean to Yourself*. San Francisco: Harper-SanFrancisco.

Beisser, Arnold R., M.D. 1991. *A Graceful Passage*. New York: Bantam Books.

Chesterton, G. K. 1988. in *1,911 Best Things Anybody Ever Said*. Edited by Robert Byrne, New York: Fawcett Columbine.

Covey, Stephen R. 1989. *The Seven Habits of Highly Effective People*. New York: Fireside/Simon & Shuster.

Einstein, Albert. 1954. *Ideas and Opinions*. New York: Bonanza Books.

Einstein, Albert. 1956. *The World As I See It/Out of My Later Years*. New York: Quality Paperback Books.

Emerson, Ralph Waldo. 1993. *Self-Reliance*. New York: Penguin Books.

Frankl, Viktor E. 1992. *Man's Search for Meaning*. Boston: Beacon Press.

Hunt, Morton. 1993. *The Story of Psychology*. New York: Doubleday.

LaRochefoucauld, Francois. in *1,911 Best Things Anybody Ever Said*. Edited by Robert Byrne, New York: Fawcett Columbine.

Leonard, George. 1991. *Mastery*. New York: Dutton.

McKay, Matthew, and Patrick Fanning. 1992. *Self-Esteem, 2d ed*. Oakland, Calif.: New Harbinger Publications.

Miller, Alice. 1991. *Breaking Down the Wall of Silence*. New York: Dutton.

Neddleman, Jacob. 1991. *Money and the Meaning of Life*. New York: Doubleday.

Ornstein, Robert, and Paul Ehrlich. 1989. *New World, New Mind*. New York: Doubleday.

Parks, Rosa, and Gregory Reed. 1994. *Quiet Strength*. Grand Rapids, Mich.: Zondervan Publishing House.

Peck, M. Scott. 1978. *The Road Less Traveled*. New York: Simon & Schuster.

Reeve, Christopher. 1998. *Still Me*. New York: Random House.

Roberts, Jane. 1974. *The Nature of Personal Reality*. New York: Bantam.

Robbins, Anthony. 1991. *Awaken the Giant Within*. New York: Summit Books.

Reynolds, David K. 1995. *A Handbook for Constructive Living*. New York: William Morrow and Company, Inc.

Rutledge, Thom. 1997. *The Self-Forgiveness Handbook*. Oakland, Calif.: New Harbinger Publications.

Rutledge, Thom. 1990. *Simple Truth*. Nashville, Tenn.: Thom Rutledge Publishing.

Stettbacher, J. Konrad. 1991. *Making Sense of Suffering*. New York: Dutton.

Subby, Robert. 1987. *Lost in the Shuffle*. Pompano Beach, Fla.: Health Communications, Inc.

Tillich, Paul. 1963. *The Eternal Now*. New York: Charles Scribner's Sons.

Tripp, Rhoda Thomas. 1987. *The International Thesaurus of Quotations*. New York: Perrenial Library.

Some Other New Harbinger Self-Help Titles

High on Stress: A Woman's Guide to Optimizing the Stress in Her Life, $13.95

Infidelity: A Survival Guide, $12.95

Stop Walking on Eggshells, $13.95

Consumer's Guide to Psychiatric Drugs, $13.95

The Fibromyalgia Advocate: Getting the Support You Need to Cope with Fibromyalgia and Myofascial Pain, $18.95

Healing Fear: New Approaches to Overcoming Anxiety, $16.95

Working Anger: Preventing and Resolving Conflict on the Job, $12.95

Sex Smart: How Your Childhood Shaped Your Sexual Life and What to Do About It, $14.95

You Can Free Yourself From Alcohol & Drugs, $13.95

Amongst Ourselves: A Self-Help Guide to Living with Dissociative Identity Disorder, $14.95

Healthy Living with Diabetes, $13.95

Dr. Carl Robinson's Basic Baby Care, $10.95

Better Boundries: Owning and Treasuring Your Life, $13.95

Goodbye Good Girl, $12.95

Being, Belonging, Doing, $10.95

Thoughts & Feelings, Second Edition, $18.95

Depression: How It Happens, How It's Healed, $14.95

Trust After Trauma, $13.95

The Chemotherapy & Radiation Survival Guide, Second Edition, $14.95

Heart Therapy, $13.95

Surviving Childhood Cancer, $12.95

The Headache & Neck Pain Workbook, $14.95

Perimenopause, $13.95

The Self-Forgiveness Handbook, $12.95

A Woman's Guide to Overcoming Sexual Fear and Pain, $14.95

Mind Over Malignancy, $12.95

Treating Panic Disorder and Agoraphobia, $44.95

Scarred Soul, $13.95

The Angry Heart, $14.95

Don't Take It Personally, $12.95

Becoming a Wise Parent For Your Grown Child, $12.95

Clear Your Past, Change Your Future, $13.95

Preparing for Surgery, $17.95

The Power of Two, $12.95

It's Not OK Anymore, $13.95

The Daily Relaxer, $12.95

The Body Image Workbook, $17.95

Living with ADD, $17.95

Taking the Anxiety Out of Taking Tests, $12.95

Five Weeks to Healing Stress: The Wellness Option, $17.95

Why Children Misbehave and What to Do About It, $14.95

When Anger Hurts Your Kids, $12.95

The Addiction Workbook, $17.95

The Chronic Pain Control Workbook, Second Edition, $17.95

Fibromyalgia & Chronic Myofascial Pain Syndrome, $19.95

Flying Without Fear, $13.95

Kid Cooperation: How to Stop Yelling, Nagging & Pleading and Get Kids to Cooperate, $13.95

The Stop Smoking Workbook: Your Guide to Healthy Quitting, $17.95

Conquering Carpal Tunnel Syndrome and Other Repetitive Strain Injuries, $17.95

An End to Panic: Breakthrough Techniques for Overcoming Panic Disorder, Second Edition, $18.95

Letting Go of Anger: The 10 Most Common Anger Styles and What to Do About Them, $12.95

Messages: The Communication Skills Workbook, Second Edition, $13.95

Coping With Chronic Fatigue Syndrome: Nine Things You Can Do, $13.95

The Anxiety & Phobia Workbook, Second Edition, $18.95

The Relaxation & Stress Reduction Workbook, Fourth Edition, $17.95

Living Without Depression & Manic Depression: A Workbook for Maintaining Mood Stability, $17.95

Coping With Schizophrenia: A Guide For Families, $15.95

Visualization for Change, Second Edition, $15.95

Postpartum Survival Guide, $13.95

Angry All the Time: An Emergency Guide to Anger Control, $12.95

Couple Skills: Making Your Relationship Work, $13.95

Self-Esteem, Second Edition, $13.95

I Can't Get Over It, A Handbook for Trauma Survivors, Second Edition, $15.95

Dying of Embarrassment: Help for Social Anxiety and Social Phobia, $13.95

The Depression Workbook: Living With Depression and Manic Depression, $17.95

Men & Grief: A Guide for Men Surviving the Death of a Loved One, $14.95

When Once Is Not Enough: Help for Obsessive Compulsives, $13.95

Beyond Grief: A Guide for Recovering from the Death of a Loved One, $13.95

Hypnosis for Change: A Manual of Proven Techniques, Third Edition, $15.95

When Anger Hurts, $13.95

Call **toll free, 1-800-748-6273,** to order. Have your Visa or Mastercard number ready. Or send a check for the titles you want to New Harbinger Publications, Inc., 5674 Shattuck Ave., Oakland, CA 94609. Include $3.80 for the first book and 75¢ for each additional book, to cover shipping and handling. (California residents please include appropriate sales tax.) Allow two to five weeks for delivery.

Prices subject to change without notice.

More New Harbinger Titles
for Personal Growth and Change

THE SELF-FORGIVENESS HANDBOOK

Guided exercises, refined over the years in Thom Rutledge's practice and motivating workshops, take you on an empowering journey from self-criticism to self-compassion and inner strength.
Item FORG $12.95

HEALING FEAR

Therapist Edmund Bourne shares the hard-won wisdom and the healing strategies that helped him recover from his own personal struggle with anxiety and attain a new serenity.   *Item HFR $16.95*

YOU CAN FREE YOURSELF FROM ALCOHOL & DRUGS

A balanced, ten-goal recovery program helps readers make needed lifestyle changes without forcing them to embrace unwelcome religious concepts or beliefs.   *Item YFDA Paperback, $13.95*

LIVING WITHOUT PROCRASTINATION

Helps you unlearn counterproductive habits, change paralyzing beliefs and attitudes, overcome resistance, develop task-directed thinking, and attain a new sense of purposefulness.
Item LWP Paperback, $12.95

DON'T TAKE IT PERSONALLY

Shows you how to depersonalize your responses to rejection, protect yourself from hurt, and develop a new sense of self-acceptance and self-confidence.   *Item DOTA Paperback $12.95*

BETTER BOUNDARIES

If you feel like you have trouble saying no to others, at work or at home, this book can help you establish more effective boundaries.
Item BB Paperback, $13.95

Call toll-free 1-800-748-6273 to order. Have your Visa or Mastercard number ready. Or send a check for the titles you want to New Harbinger Publications, 5674 Shattuck Avenue, Oakland, CA 94609. Include $3.80 for the first book and 75¢ for each additional book to cover shipping and handling. (California residents please include appropriate sales tax.) Allow four to six weeks for delivery.

Prices subject to change without notice.